Dry Tortugas National Park Vegetation Map, 2009

Natural Resource Technical Report NPS/SFCN/NRTR—2011/469

Jose M. Luciani[1, 2]
Resource Management Intern

Kevin R. T. Whelan, Ph.D.[2]
Community Ecologist

Robert B. Shamblin[2]
Botanist

Rachel M. Vargas[2]
Data Management/Outreach Specialist

Judd M. Patterson[2]
GIS Specialist

[1]Florida International University
Southeast Environmental Research Center
University Park Campus
Miami, FL 33199

[2]National Park Service
South Florida / Caribbean Network
18001 Old Cutler Rd., Suite 419
Village of Palmetto Bay, FL 33157

July 2011

U.S. Department of the Interior
National Park Service
Natural Resource Stewardship and Science
Fort Collins, Colorado

The National Park Service, Natural Resource Stewardship and Science office in Fort Collins, Colorado publishes a range of reports that address natural resource topics of interest and applicability to a broad audience in the National Park Service and others in natural resource management, including scientists, conservation and environmental constituencies, and the public.

The Natural Resource Technical Report Series is used to disseminate results of scientific studies in the physical, biological, and social sciences for both the advancement of science and the achievement of the National Park Service mission. The series provides contributors with a forum for displaying comprehensive data that are often deleted from journals because of page limitations.

All manuscripts in the series receive the appropriate level of peer review to ensure that the information is scientifically credible, technically accurate, appropriately written for the intended audience, and designed and published in a professional manner. This report received formal peer review by subject-matter experts who were not directly involved in the collection, analysis, or reporting of the data, and whose background and expertise put them on par technically and scientifically with the authors of the information.

Views, statements, findings, conclusions, recommendations, and data in this report do not necessarily reflect views and policies of the National Park Service, U.S. Department of the Interior. Mention of trade names or commercial products does not constitute endorsement or recommendation for use by the U.S. Government.

This report is available from the South Florida / Caribbean Network website (http://science.nature.nps.gov/im/units/sfcn/) and the Natural Resource Publications Management website (http://www.nature.nps.gov/publications/nrpm/).

Please cite this publication as:

Luciani, J. M., K. R. T. Whelan, R. B. Shamblin, R. M. Vargas, J. M. Patterson. 2011. Dry Tortugas National Park vegetation map, 2009. Natural Resource Technical Report NPS/SFCN/NRTR—2011/469. National Park Service, Fort Collins, Colorado.

NPS 364/108143, July 2011

Contents

Figures

Tables

Appendices

Project Summary

The National Park Service Vegetation Mapping Inventory Program (NPS-VMP) funded the NPS South Florida / Caribbean Network (SFCN) to map the seven islands of Dry Tortugas National Park in 2009. The vegetation map of Dry Tortugas National Park was created by in-field polygon delineation instead of the more common photointerpretation of aerial imagery. Using the Trimble GeoXT GPS device in the field allowed the production of a finely detailed vegetation map (vegetation census) for Loggerhead Key, Garden Key, Bush Key, East Key, Long Key, Middle Key, and Hospital Key. The Dry Tortugas vegetation maps were made using the Universal Transverse Mercator (UTM) zone 17 North coordinate system and the North American Datum of 1983 (NAD 83) with a minimum mapping unit of 25 m². The SFCN developed a vegetation classification in congruence with the vegetation map of Dry Tortugas National Park. The Dry Tortugas vegetation classification conforms to the Rutchey *et al.* (2006) South Florida Vegetation Classification System coupled with the vegetation communities unique to the Dry Tortugas.

The final vegetation map has a total of 41 mapping classes and 438 polygons with a total land area of 39.4 hectares. At the physiognomic level, Dry Tortugas vegetation map included 3 Woodland classes, 8 Shrubland classes, 5 Scrub classes, 20 Dune classes, 3 Sparse Vegetation classes, and 2 Non-Vegetative classes.

Table Summary. Percentage of area covered by each physiognomic class (broken down by each individual island) and total area (ha) for each island and for all the islands combined

Class/Island	Bush	East	Garden	Hospital	Loggerhead	Long	Middle	All
Woodland	0%	0%	3.3%	0%	0%	11.5%	0%	1.1%
Shrubland	6.6%	0%	0.1%	0%	19.6%	1.5%	0%	11%
Scrub	0.2%	0%	0%	0%	0.2%	0.6%	0%	0.1%
Dune	54.6%	0.4%	12.9%	0%	38.4%	19.2%	0%	31.7%
Sparse	38%	99.6%	7.2%	100%	34.4%	67.2%	100%	34.8%
Non-Vegetative	0.6%	0%	76.5%	0%	7.4%	0%	0%	21.3%
Total Area (ha)	6.4 ha	2.3 ha	9 ha	0.4 ha	19.8 ha	1.1 ha	0.4 ha	39.4 ha

Sparse vegetation accounts for 34.8% of the entire land area in the park consisting of low to zero cover of vegetation. Non-Vegetative areas are places in the park where permanent structures have been introduced such as Fort Jefferson and Loggerhead Lighthouse that have a mixture of native and exotic vegetation on the disturbed grounds surrounding the structures. Dune associative communities are the main physiognomic classes pertaining to native communities which have significant cover on four of the seven islands. These are the most diverse physiognomic classes with 20 individual associations that are common to rare in the park. Shrubland classes constitute only 11% of the total land area which are more commonly found on Loggerhead Key and less so on Bush Key. Woodland and Scrub classes are even less common in the park. Woodland classes are restricted to Garden Key on the grounds outside Fort Jefferson and the mangroves of Long Key. The vegetation communities as they are represented on these islands differ in distribution and commonality. Some classes are only found on one island, whereas, many can be found on more than one with differences in abundance and composition.

SFCN established a cooperative agreement with Florida International University for the Resource Management Intern Program with one deliverable being the development of a vegetation map of Dry Tortugas National Park. This report is a deliverable under task agreement #J2117072808 and cooperative agreement #H5000060104.

Also included are: detailed maps of close-up sections of Loggerhead Key, Bush Key, and Long Key, historical maps from reference literature, and the field data sheet.

Acknowledgments

We wish to acknowledge the NPS National Vegetation Mapping Inventory Program for the funding of this project. We gratefully acknowledge the assistance of Tony Pernas, NPS Florida / Caribbean Exotic Plant Management Team Coordinator, Jimi Sadle, Park Botanist for Dry Tortugas and Everglades National Park, and Gary Davis, retired Ocean Science Chief for the National Park Service, for review of the resulting product. We like to thank Jimi Sadle for his assistance during the mapping effort of Loggerhead Key and for his insight. We also like to thank Tony Pernas for his insight and experience shared relating to the exotic plant activity at Dry Tortugas. We gratefully acknowledge the assistance of Dry Tortugas park staff for project logistics such as Dave Walton, site manager for Dry Tortugas, Tree Gottshall, maintenance mechanical supervisor, and Kayla Nimmo, biological technician. We would like to thank Bonnie Ciolino, archivist for Everglades National Park, for her help in searching for historical reference literature in the Everglades archive library. In addition, we express our appreciation to Dr. James Fourqurean of Florida International University for providing the Resource Management Intern for this project. Finally, this project was greatly assisted by the efforts of Joaquin Alonso, Andrea Atkinson, Tim Fotinos, and Jonathan Moser of the SFCN staff.

Introduction

Introduction to Dry Tortugas National Park

Dry Tortugas National Park, established in 1992, is one of the unique areas of our National Park System due to extensive marine life, unique barrier island ecosystems, and the largest American coastal masonry fort of the 19th century. Dry Tortugas, comprised mostly of marine systems, consists of a cluster of seven coral reef and sand islands, surrounded by shoals and submerged resources such as coral reefs and seagrass beds, forming an atoll-like bank. Dry Tortugas encompasses 264 square kilometers and comprises the westernmost part of the Florida Keys and is part of an ancient coral reef tract that extends 354 kilometers from Miami (Pernas *et al.* 2001). The 26,540 hectare park is located about 110 km (~70 miles) west of Key West, Florida, in the Straits of Florida. With about 99.9% of the park underwater, the coral and carbonate sand islands of the Dry Tortugas encompass about 39 hectares (0.1% of the park).

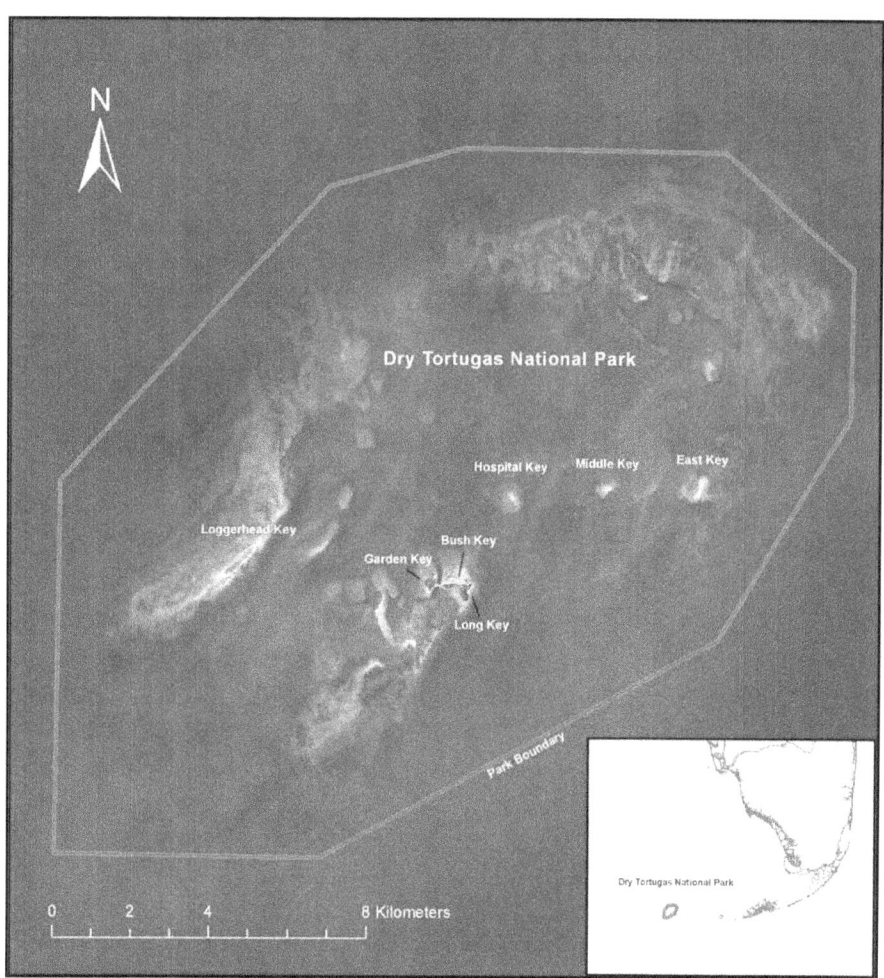

Figure 1. Dry Tortugas area map (2003 NOAA Aerial Imagery)

The islands in the park are situated on the edge of the main shipping channel between the Gulf of Mexico, the Western Caribbean, and the Atlantic Ocean. The islands and reefs pose a serious navigation hazard to ships passing through the 120-kilometer-wide straits and have been the site

1

of hundreds of shipwrecks, with some vessels dating back to the 17th century. The shipwrecks on the reefs comprise one of the nation's principal ship graveyards. These submerged cultural resources support a habitat for marine organisms to flourish. The tropical coral reefs of the Dry Tortugas are among the best developed on the continent and possess a full range of Caribbean coral species, some of which are listed as threatened, such as *Acropora cervicornis* and *Acropora palmatta*.

History of the Dry Tortugas

First visited by Ponce De Leon in 1513, the Spanish explorer named the islands "Las Tortugas" due to the large concentration of sea turtles on the Dry Tortugas bank. Las Tortugas was later changed to the Dry Tortugas to inform mariners of the lack of freshwater on these islands (Pendleton *et al.* 2005). In the centuries following the discovery of the Dry Tortugas by Ponce de Leon, the safe natural harbor of the Dry Tortugas was used by many Spanish, British, and other vessels for safe anchorage during storms (NPS 1994). Also, during this time, pirates and privateers used the Tortugas islands as a prime location to launch attacks against merchant vessels in the nearby shipping channels throughout the 17th and 18th centuries (NPS 1994).

The Tortugas came under possession of the British after Spain ceded Florida to Great Britain in 1763 (NPS 1994). The British possessed the Tortugas for the next 20 years. During 1773-1775, the islands were surveyed by George Gauld (1790), who created the first modern marine chart of the Dry Tortugas including ten islands. Of the ten islands named by Gauld, only four islands stayed with the same name throughout the centuries (East Key, Loggerhead Key, North Key, and Southwest Key). In 1783, Great Britain relinquished possession of Florida back over to Spain due to Great Britain's defeat during the American Revolutionary War (NPS 1994). Florida was in Spanish hands until 1821, when in accordance with the Adams-Onis Treaty, the United States gained possession of Florida (NPS 1994).

Following the War of 1812, the United States undertook efforts to fortify its entire coastline from Maine to Texas. At first, military occupation of the Dry Tortugas seemed impractical and impossible. On January 19, 1825, Commodore Porter took a voyage through the Dry Tortugas to explore the idea of a military presence on the islands. He stated in a letter back to the Secretary of the Navy that "...examining the Dry Tortugas which I find totally unfit for any kind of Naval establishment" (Roth, date unknown). However, that same year, a lighthouse would be erected on Garden Key. The lighthouse was authorized and completed three years after the Congressional Act of May 7, 1822, thus establishing the first permanent structure on these islands (Roth, date unknown). The lighthouse erected on Garden Key signifies some measure of importance of the Dry Tortugas and their position for the success of American commerce in the Gulf of Mexico and the Caribbean. In 1829, Lieutenants Josiah Tatnall and G.R. Gednery, with orders from President Andrew Jackson to survey the Dry Tortugas, charted the island chain with areas and elevations for six of the eleven islands then present (Robertson 1964). Lt. Tatnall recommended the Dry Tortugas for its military practicability in protecting commerce, gaining position, and general rendezvous and concentration for all operations in the area (Roth, date unknown). Military presence in the Dry Tortugas never came to fruition until Florida became the 27th state of the Union on March 3, 1845. The next day, James Knox Polk was inaugurated the 11th President of the United States. On July 24th, Florida legislature "passed an act enabling transfer of lands to the U.S. for military purposes" (Roth, date unknown). On September 17, 1845, the Dry Tortugas was given jurisdiction to the U.S. by Florida (Roth, date unknown). That same day, President Polk gave an executive order creating a military reservation on the Dry Tortugas (Roth, date unknown). Immediately before construction began in 1846 on Fort Jefferson, "Major Hartman Bache completed a topographic survey of the islands" (Roth, date unknown). Unfortunately, this detailed topographic map had limited usefulness because an October hurricane changed the contour of Garden Key. Garden Key was chosen as the site of the fort instead of the larger Loggerhead Key, because Garden Key has an advantageous location near the Tortugas harbor.

Fort Jefferson, on Garden Key, is the park's central cultural feature and one of the largest American coastal forts, and a "militarily and architecturally significant 19th century fort" (NPS 1999). Construction began on the structure in 1846, but the fort was never completed. Many difficulties were encountered during the fort's construction that led to its incompletion. The main reasons were funding difficulties and extraordinary logistical problems (NPS 1994). The construction of the fort was finally discontinued when the introduction of the rifled cannon made the fort's defenses obsolete because of the penetrating ability of the weapon (NPS 1994). During 1856-1860, the lighthouse on Garden Key was reduced to a harbor light when a taller lighthouse was erected on Loggerhead Key (Roth, date unknown). During and after the Civil War, originally built to protect shipping access to the Gulf, the fort was used as a military prison, housing Union deserters and four Lincoln assassination conspirators. Due to fever outbreaks and hurricane damage, the fort was abandoned in 1874 (NPS 1994). Thereafter, the fort would be reoccupied multiple times. It was once used as a coaling station, where two coaling docks were constructed outside the fort walls, and as a seaplane base during World War I (NPS 1994). However, without military presence, storms and salvagers took a toll on the fort until it became a National Monument on January 4, 1935.

The Dry Tortugas has been the subject of important historical research in its long history. Alexander Agassiz studied coral reef resources extensively during the late 19th century. Agassiz mapped the Dry Tortugas coral reef tract communities in 1881, and was published in 1883 (Agassiz 1883). In 1904, Loggerhead Key was the site of the Carnegie Institution of Washington D.C., a marine laboratory publishing 35 volumes of research data spanning 36 years in the Dry Tortugas (NPS 1994). Although pioneers in the field of tropical marine science, their presence had a profound effect on the native vegetation on Loggerhead Key which would be evident in the decades to come after their departure.

System Drivers and Stressors

The Dry Tortugas has a sub-tropical climate with warm moist summers and dry winters. "Mean daily temperature ranges from 21.3°C in January to 29.1°C in August" (Stoddart and Fosberg 1981). During the hurricane season (June-November), the Dry Tortugas experiences both hot, humid weather and calm seas or severe weather events, which can bring heavy rainfall, high winds and storm surge. Summer temperatures can reach record maximum temperatures in the upper 90s. The winter dry season is usually windy with rough seas. The winters can see cold spells that last several days. As a result, the hot climate coupled with little available standing freshwater leads to dry tropical and sub-tropical vegetation community composition that is adapted to such extreme conditions. The vegetation also needs to withstand salt spray and salt water inundation during severe storm events. Severe weather events such as hurricanes not only inundate the low topography of the islands but damage vegetation and move the actual soil of the islands causing mortality and shifts in species composition. This is due in large part to massive substrate disturbance, salt stress, and physical damage to plants caused by these large storm events. The mortality of vegetation communities due to hurricanes often resets the vegetation succession processes. However, the ability of native vegetation to re-colonize after such a stressor is an adaptation of many of the pioneer coastal species present on the islands.

The Dry Tortugas is not a place of stability but one of change. There are occasional floristic changes from storms, and the islands themselves are continually altered. A single storm event can shift sand from one beach and deposit it on another (Thornberry-Ehrlich 2005). The islands' shapes and profiles are constantly changing. Some islands have disappeared altogether, such as Bird Key, Northeast Key, North Key, and Southwest Key. Aside from tropical systems, sea level rise is gradually inundating these low lying islands, although storm deposits could offset this. Currently, Middle Key is submerged seasonally due to the thermal expansion of the ocean causing sea level rise at the end of the summer. The islands within Dry Tortugas with the highest rates of shoreline erosion and the highest wave energy are most at risk, such as Hospital Key, Middle Key, and East Key (Pendleton *et al.* 2005). Dry Tortugas National Park may eventually lose more islands over this century if deposition processes do not keep pace. "The areas least vulnerable to sea-level rise may be the south facing shorelines of Bush and Long Key due to shoreline accretion and low wave energy" (Pendleton *et al.* 2005). Sea level rise will also impact the more stable larger islands in the park where shoreline erosion will alter turtle nesting habitats and cause shrinking of island areas where colonial bird nesting habitat maybe affected.

Exotic vegetation is another stressor that impacts the composition of native floral species at Dry Tortugas. Loggerhead Key and Garden Key have been subject to years of human impact, thus introduction of exotic vegetation occurred more readily. Although Garden Key has seen the highest number of introduced exotic species, the flora of Loggerhead Key was more heavily affected by the introduction of *Casuarina equisetifolia* and *Agave* spp. *Casuarina* was introduced around 1910 by the director of the Carnegie Institution (Stoddart and Fosberg 1981). *Casuarina* would eventually spread throughout the entire island, which became a forest with an understory of *Agave* spp. until restoration efforts removed the invasive community in the 1990s (Pernas *et al.* 2001).

Vegetation Communities

There have been five valuable vegetation studies that have produced historical vegetation records and vegetation maps of the seven current islands. They are listed in Schmidt's bibliography of scientific studies done in Dry Tortugas National park (1997). These studies include Millspaugh (1907), Bowman (1918), Davis (1942), Schroeder (1971) and Stoddart and Fosberg (1981). Their historical reports identified vegetation communities present in the Dry Tortugas. The historical reports used ecological terms like "associes" and "consocies." The terms are included in the current report to describe the authors' findings, but these terms are not used in the 2009 vegetation classification. "Associes" and "consocies" are terms used to describe a community's developmental stage and composition. "Associes" indicates that the dominant vegetation has other associated species present within the community. "Consocies" are primarily communities made up of a single dominant species. In addition, "consocies" may suggest a near climax community. It is important to state that this report does not try to replicate the method of classifying vegetation from these previous studies. The historical reports are a valuable and vital source of the past communities and their location in Dry Tortugas National Park.

Millspaugh's report was based on accounts from the 1904 surveys of O.E. Lansing, Jr. In the report of Millspaugh (1907), the author described the distribution of species on five of the eight islands then present. Millspaugh didn't describe any vegetation communities or associations that were found but did explain the spatial distribution and commonality of each species. One definite community, the *Suriana* community, can be interpreted from his description of Loggerhead Key and Bird Key and their vegetation maps (Appendix C, p. 97). The historical reports following Millspaugh (1907) described commonly found communities on the islands. According to Stoddart and Fosberg, Bowman described four associations: the *Uniola* community, the *Suriana* community, the *Opuntia* community, and the *Chamaesyce* community. Bowman used these four associations to describe the vegetation present on the eight islands in the Dry Tortugas, but was not limited by this general classification of the vegetation. Among these communities, Bowman further described smaller vegetative associations or lesser communities, such as groups, patches, or colonies, found within these main communities (Appendix C, pp. 99-103). Although Bowman described communities within his report, the vegetation maps give detailed locations for many species and lack any generalization of vegetation.

At a greater level of detail, Davis explained three disjunctive "topographic units common to the Florida Keys" (Fosberg and Stoddart 1981) in order to organize the vegetation into feature classes. These units were mainly used to describe the type of environment the community was found in. Strand-beach associes, including such species as *Sesuvium, Cakile, Ipomoea, Sporobolus, Uniola, Chamaesyce,* and *Argusia* (Fosberg and Stoddart 1981), were mainly found in a scattered, mostly open sand beach environment with scattered individuals/small groups of colonies or families (Davis 1942). Usually, the dominant species in a particular environment precedes the topographic description of the community. Strand-dune associes, including such species as *Uniola, Chamaesyce, Hymenocallis, Argusia,* and *Suriana,* existed in the interior dunes. The strand-scrub associes mostly consist of the sub-climax *Suriana* consocies. Davis distinguished seven major communities: strand-beach associes, *Uniola* strand-dune associes, *Suriana* consocies, *Opuntia* associes, *Chamaesyce* associes, *Agave* associes, and *Laguncularia* associes (Davis 1942). These communities are exhibited in Davis's vegetation map as polygons on Loggerhead Key, Garden Key, Bush Key, and Long Key. Davis was the first author to illustrate the vegetation communities on the map as polygons (Appendix C, p. 104). Within the polygons, Davis illustrated spatial distribution of other associative species found within these communities. According to Davis, the other species were "scattered individuals of the strand-beach and strand-dune associes, forming at most small colonies" (Davis 1942). Davis did separate smaller distinct communities, as Bowman did, but they are not as ubiquitous as the common *Suriana* consocies, *Chamaesyce* associes, *Uniola* strand-dune associes, and *Sesuvium* consocies. Davis's efforts to map the sand islands of Dry Tortugas forced him to lump many species, which may have formed small communities, because of the mapping restrictions of the time. Lastly, Stoddart and Fosberg agreed with the vegetative nomenclature of the Dry Tortugas but they suggested a new *Casuarina* woodland unit was necessary (Appendix C, pp. 105-107). This *Casuarina* class is no longer present due to the eradication of the exotic vegetation by the National Park Service in 2001. The vegetation maps of Stoddart and Fosberg also represent a generalization of the vegetation communities of Dry Tortugas.

Methods

Project Overview

The current Dry Tortugas National Park vegetation map was generated by a Resource Monitoring Intern through a cooperative agreement between Florida International University and the South Florida / Caribbean Inventory and Monitoring Network (SFCN) of the National Park Service. The Resource Monitoring Intern created the map polygons with the assistance of the SFCN community ecology staff and the data management staff. SFCN staff conducted the field data collection, analysis and vegetation classification development. The map was created by in-field polygon creation (each community edge was walked with a Trimble GeoXT) and post-field cleanup of polygon edges, thus, no photointerpretation of imagery was done. The vegetation and shoreline of Loggerhead Key, Bush Key, Long Key, Garden Key, Hospital Key, Middle Key, and East Key were all mapped. SFCN consulted with park resource management staff and received considerable assistance with logistical support, important references, and review of the resulting map. The SFCN staff developed vegetation types of the floral communities present on the islands. A list of the various vegetation types was formulated throughout all the islands (Table 11, p. 49). The vegetation types were developed, following the field, into vegetation classes to follow the South Florida classification system (Rutchey *et al.* 2006) and for those classes which are unique to Dry Tortugas National Park (Table 6, pp. 41-42). The project was initially funded in 2009, work began in earnest in June 2009, and was completed in May 2010.

Creation of Field Data Sheets and Preparation of Trimble GeoXT

The Dry Tortugas vegetation mapping data sheet was created to collect the following data: island mapped, observers, date in which the polygons were made, Garmin 60 CSx unit number used and the GPS waypoint number, dominant vegetation type of the polygon (written as a number code), the quantity of pictures associated with the polygon, species present within the polygon, and any comments about the polygon composition or polygon shape (Appendix D, p. 109). The vegetation type code number is related to a specific vegetation type described by the dominant species found in the vegetation community (Table 11, p. 49). The description of these vegetation type codes were created in-situ after an initial walk through the island, with the option to add vegetation types as encountered.

The GPS devices that were used to field delineate vegetation polygons were the Trimble GeoXT and the Trimble GeoXT 2005 series. Both Trimble devices were used with the internal antennae. The Trimble GeoXT was configured to collect line features of the polygons. A feature name menu was created to separate shoreline polygon from a vegetation polygon. A Trimble program called Data Dictionary Editor was used to add attributes in the Terrasync program on the Trimble GeoXT which allows field attributes to show up at each new polygon. A drop-down list of each attribute helped with efficient data entry in the field. The following five fields were used on the Trimble GeoXT at each new vegetation polygon: veg type, Garmin GPS unit, Garmin GPS mark, observer, and comments.

Collection of Field Data

All vegetation polygons were created via hiking, traversing each island until all vegetation communities had been mapped and recorded. When a community was reached that clearly was distinguishable from adjacent vegetation communities, this area was mapped using the Trimble GeoXT. Consequently, the polygon outlined the extent of these vegetation communities. The two person field team consisted of a delineator with the Trimble unit and a data recorder. The delineator carefully walked the edge of the vegetation community and delineated the polygon location. With the Trimble unit on and the Terrasync program opened, the delineator was able to create a polygon and assign attributes associated with that particular polygon. Meanwhile, the data recorder was used to take a GPS waypoint on a Garmin 60 CSx (at the start location which was temporarily marked with a pvc pole) and in combination with the Garmin 60 CSx unit number created a unique identifier for the polygon and associated data. An initial photograph was taken of the data sheet followed by a number of pictures of the dominant vegetation comprising the polygon along with any unique species. Some features were mapped that are not vegetation communities but were considered to be important features like sand patches between vegetation polygons, coral rubble on Bush Key and Long Key, and an ephemeral salt pond on Bush Key. In general, we began mapping at the edges of the island and worked our way inland.

The shoreline of each island was walked to create a shoreline polygon on the Trimble unit, except for Loggerhead Key, where a Garmin 60 CSx unit was used to map the shoreline. The Garmin created a trackline which was converted to a shapefile polygon. Shoreline was defined as the water line at the time the island was walked. On Hospital, Middle, and East Keys, two dune elevations (secondary and crown dune) were also mapped. These features were considered the more stable parts of these smaller islands. At the end of the day, all the data that were collected on the Trimble GeoXT, Garmin 60 CSx, and field cameras were downloaded onto a laptop. This backup served as a secondary source in case of electronic malfunction or damage.

Database Design and Creation

Following the mapping effort, all the data collected on the GPS units, cameras, and data sheets were downloaded and organized on a computer. Garmin 60 CSx data were downloaded, separated by unit, and given a download date (e.g., Garmin60_1_2009XXXX_waypoints). Each Trimble GeoXT was downloaded through the GPS Pathfinder Office program. First, the Trimble GeoXT was connected via a type B USB connection cable to the computer. Under the Trimble program list, the Datatransfer program was opened. This program transferred the GPS data in the Trimble to the computer as .ssf files. Subsequently, the GPS Pathfinder Office program converted these .ssf files to .cor files. This was accomplished by differentially correcting the .ssf files. The GPS Pathfinder Office selects the .ssf files just retrieved from the Trimble unit. The files were differentially corrected by selecting the Continually Operating Reference Station (CORS) site closest to the Dry Tortugas – in this case, the Key West CORS site. This process created a .cor file with improved horizontal accuracy. This file was exported as a shapefile. Before viewing or editing of the shapefile, a new personal geodatabase was created under the appropriate folder. The shapefile containing the Dry Tortugas polygons was imported into the geodatabase using ArcCatalog. The file, which was now in its new output location, was added in ArcMap. Once in ArcMap GIS, the shapefile could be viewed, edited, and attributed further.

Data entry into Excel was done for the first mapping trip. An Excel spreadsheet with the same fields from the field data sheets was created. The data were entered into this Excel spreadsheet with the intention of joining the spreadsheet with the Dry Tortugas polygon attribute table. This was done by adding a new field column called unit_mark in both the ArcMap GIS attribute table and in the Excel spreadsheet. While using a command in Excel and ArcMap, the Garmin unit number and mark number was combined (e.g., 1_058). This would be known as the unique identifier. In ArcMap, the Excel spreadsheet was joined using the unique identifier as the link to match data to the correct rows. To make the join permanent, the new attribute table needed to be exported as a new feature class within the geodatabase.

Data entry for the second mapping trip was entered directly into Microsoft Access. Previously entered data from Microsoft Excel was imported at the same time. The unique identifier was also used to link the Access database. The database entry forms possessed the same fields found on the data sheet. A unique identifier entry field linked the Access database to the attribute table but also helped organize data entry. Once all the data had been entered in the Access database, the many polygon photos that were taken in the field could now be linked to their specific polygons in the database. A ThumbsPlus 7 database was used to catalog all photos taken during the field campaigns, allowing data from field data sheets to be digitally associated with each individual photo. These data relationships allow for the development of an ArcMap project that shows vegetation data and field photographs together.

Refinement and Finalization of Polygons

When the polygons were brought into ArcMap for the first time, they had many jagged edges resulting from the Trimble GeoXT having a logging interval of every second and a variable GPS signal strength. Inconsistencies in polygons were fixed by post-process in ArcMap GIS. Polygons are made up of vertices which can be moved, deleted, or added in order to re-shape them. Any movement of the vertices during the cleanup was minimal compared to the original shape of the polygons. To speed up field delineation of vegetation polygons, sometimes there was a comment written on the data sheet instructing use of the edge of a different polygon. In ArcMap, the vertices were moved to the edge given priority. The polygon edge that was brought over was then clipped to remove any overlap. Some comments on the data sheet included combining similar polygons into one. In ArcMap's editor function, the merge tool combined these similar polygons into one. Merging of polygons occurred only with comparable polygons close to one another which had no other polygons impeding their merger. Lastly, while the delineator was walking a polygon edge, sometimes a certain portion of the edge was impassable or led straight to the polygon start point. The delineator proceeded to make a snapline of the polygon edge straight to where he/she began walking the edge. The data recorder noted in the field which polygon edge to use and this was corrected in ArcMap using the clip tool.

Clipping took place when the data recorder mentioned to use a certain edge or if two polygons overlapped, but also when there was a polygon within a larger polygon with no mention of edges. There were some instances where a small polygon needed to be clipped out of a larger enveloping polygon. Typically, in the field, smaller vegetation polygons had very detailed edges and these were clipped out of larger vegetation polygons.

Some areas were not mapped to a specified polygon but were noted in the field and were added in office as an area between mapped polygons. Photos and field notes helped with placing added polygons in a definite area. Although not mapped with the Trimble GeoXT, the added polygons do have data associated with them such as the vegetation type and the species present within this community. Some of these features that were added have little to no vegetation; instead they are areas of coral rubble and an ephemeral salt pond. All polygons were double checked to corroborate the vegetation types with photos and the field data sheets before all polygons were merged into one final layer. Furthermore, the data on the attribute table was cross checked with the field data sheets.

For each of the three trips to the Dry Tortugas, the data and polygons were worked on individually and later merged together into a collective map. Once the map was whole, polygons overlapped slightly or had small gaps between polygons. To check for any errors, such as slivers or overlaps in the vegetation shapefile, we did a topology check. In order to do this we created a new feature dataset in the Geodatabase and brought in the latest merged vegetation map shapefile. We created a topology within the feature dataset and imported this shapefile. The rules were set to find and mark any gaps or overlaps within the shapefile. Each error was checked and fixed accordingly. When there was an overlap, a decision was made as to which polygon received the overlapping section. The decision was based on data sheet notes and photos on those particular vegetation polygons. If there was a gap between polygons, a new polygon was created to fill in the gap. Sometimes, depending on the size, this gap was an unmapped polygon specified on the field data sheet as being a certain vegetation type. However, this new polygon was usually only a very small gap that needed to be merged with a bordering polygon.

Vegetation Classification

The National Vegetation Classification System (NVCS) hierarchy is currently under revision for the natural areas of South Florida. SFCN used the vegetation classification for South Florida natural areas (Rutchey *et al.* 2006) as a basis for the Dry Tortugas vegetation classification. The Rutchey *et al.* (2006) document provides a hierarchical classification system, up to six levels, with more specific descriptions of the vegetation class the lower the level (e.g., level 6). "The different levels of this classification system represent distinctions in ecological communities, taxonomy, individual species, and physical characteristics such as density and height" (Rutchey *et al.* 2006). This document provides a good identification of vegetation communities in South Florida natural areas, but does not describe effectively the vegetation in Dry Tortugas National Park. Thus, from the mapping efforts in 2009, SFCN developed a Dry Tortugas vegetation classification that incorporates material from Rutchey *et al.* (2006) but adds proposed Dry Tortugas Formations/Sub-formations, Alliances, and Associations described by SFCN. Vegetation communities were categorized in the following hierarchy:

Vegetation Physiognomic Class (NVCS)
    South Florida Formation / Dry Tortugas Formation (Rutchey *et al.* 2006 or SFCN)
        South Florida Sub-formation / Dry Tortugas Sub-formation (Rutchey *et al.* 2006 or SFCN)
            Alliance/Association (SFCN)

Six vegetation physiognomic classes (Woodland, Shrubland, Scrub, Dune, Sparse Vegetation, and Non-Vegetative) were used as broad divisions of classification. Most of the physiognomic classes were taken from Rutchey *et al.* (2006), which was taken from NVCS. However, Sparse Vegetation is a NVCS physiognomic class not used in Rutchey *et al.* (2006), but is used in the vegetation classification for the Dry Tortugas. Overall, the Dry Tortugas vegetation classification uses 10 South Florida Formations and 13 South Florida Sub-formations from Rutchey *et al.* (2006). Although these Formations and Sub-formations do describe some of the higher levels of vegetation hierarchy in the Dry Tortugas, the Rutchey *et al.* (2006) descriptions for the Formations/Sub-formations are a generalized depiction and do not specifically represent the Dry Tortugas vegetation encountered during field work. For these reasons, the lower levels below South Florida Sub-formations are unique Associations or Alliances found in Dry Tortugas. The Dry Tortugas vegetation classification is given in Table 6 (pp. 41-42) with the notation "S. Fla"

(South Florida) representing classes derived from Rutchey *et al.* (2006) and the notation "DRTO" representing classes developed by SFCN.
For example:

I. Woodland (S. Fla)

    A. Mangrove Woodland (S. Fla)

       1. Black Mangrove Woodland (S. Fla)

          Avicennia germinans Woodland (DRTO)

The Black Mangrove Woodland found in the Dry Tortugas is different from the Black Mangrove Woodland level in Rutchey *et al.* (2006), in which it describes a more generalized community found elsewhere besides Dry Tortugas. SFCN gives a description for all site specific vegetation classes that were used to map the Dry Tortugas. Thus, an additional 3 Dry Tortugas Formations (Sparse Vegetation-Sand, Beach, and Coral Rubble) and 17 Dry Tortugas Sub-formations were created by SFCN to define communities that were absent in Rutchey *et al.* (2006). Thirty Associations and six Alliances were defined by SFCN with descriptions of the characteristic vegetation and environment that were encountered during the creation of this vegetation map project.

Appendix A (pp. 57-90) provides the vegetation classification key and descriptions of 3 Dry Tortugas Formations, 2 Dry Tortugas Sub-formations, 30 Associations, and 6 Alliances, including:

Alliance/Association Name:	Name using scientific names
Name, translated:	Name using common names
Vegetation:	Describes dominant/co-dominant species at Dry Tortugas National Park. Other characteristic species, canopy height and canopy cover are also included.
Environment:	Describes location/environment of the community at Dry Tortugas National Park

The Dry Tortugas Formations / Sub-formations, Associations, and Alliances described in this report are considered provisional as they have not been officially accepted into the National Vegetation Classification System at this time. This report makes no attempt to extrapolate ranges beyond Dry Tortugas National Park or make assumptions about other species that might be present at other places. SFCN assumes that the detailed formatting and descriptions necessary to complete descriptions for the National Vegetation Classification System will be provided separately by the NPS Vegetation Mapping Inventory Program once the NVCS revisions are complete for South Florida.

Results

During the first field mapping effort in June 2009, the following islands were mapped: Loggerhead Key, Hospital Key, Middle Key, East Key, and Garden Key. In October 2009, Bush Key and Long Key were mapped. Additionally, some minor locations were checked on Loggerhead. Some minor checks were also performed on Garden Key in May 2010. For simplicity, we refer to each trip according to the month the mapping took place. A list of 35 vegetation types was developed across all islands. The vegetation types were used mainly in the field to identify the dominant flora in communities with a description on the data sheet of the canopy height and canopy cover. Later, the vegetation types were placed into classes that conform to the South Florida classification system (Rutchey *et al.* 2006) and those which are unique to the Dry Tortugas. The vegetation classes were also based on community structure. There are a total of 41 mapping classes: there are 3 Woodland classes, 8 Shrubland classes, 5 Scrub classes, 20 Dune classes, 3 Sparse Vegetation classes, and 2 Non-Vegetative classes. Collectively, all the class polygons accrue to a total of 438 polygons across seven islands. At 39.37 ha (97.28 acres), the polygons cover the entire land area of Dry Tortugas National Park. Of the total 438 polygons, 113 are smaller than the minimum mapping unit of 25 m². For a listing of all the vegetation classes and their areas, refer to Table 6 (pp. 41-42) and Table 7 (pp. 43-45).

Loggerhead Key

At 19.75 ha (48.81 acres), Loggerhead Key (Figure 2, p. 18 and Appendix B, pp. 91-92) is the largest island in the park. A total of 145 polygons were created on this island: 138 polygons from the June trip and 7 polygons from the October trip. A total of 24 vegetation classes were used to identify communities on Loggerhead Key. The 24 vegetation classes (Table 1, p.14) consist of 6 Shrubland classes, 1 Scrub class, 14 Dune classes, 2 Sparse Vegetation classes, and 1 Non-Vegetative class.

The largest vegetation community on Loggerhead Key is *Opuntia stricta-Ipomoea alba* Dune Alliance which covers 2.39 ha (12.1%) of the island. The second most common vegetation community is *Argusia gnaphalodes* Shrubland at 2.23 ha (11.3%). The Beach cover class constitutes 5.37 ha (27.1%) of the island. Loggerhead Key has a wide southeastern beach. This leads into either Sparse Vegetation-Sand and/or *Argusia gnaphalodes* Shrubland, which fringes the southeastern border of the island.

South of the lighthouse area, the southern extent of vegetation is mostly made up of a large community of *Iva imbricata-Chamaesyce mesembrianthemifolia-Uniola paniculata* Dune Alliance. Beyond the vegetation, the southwest tip has a wide Beach area. South of this, a spit of beach extends southwestward and then curves west. This spit varies with the season but has an inclination to curve westerly.

For the middle interior of Loggerhead Key, *Suriana maritima* Shrubland and *Opuntia stricta* Dune Association are more prominent south of the lighthouse than north of it. This middle interior also has sizable polygons of *Opuntia stricta-Ipomoea alba* Dune Alliance and *Ipomoea alba* Dune Association. The area south of the lighthouse ends with a western border mostly dominated by *Suriana maritima* Shrubland, *Argusia gnaphalodes* Shrubland, *Uniola paniculata* Dune Association, and *Opuntia stricta-Ipomoea alba* Dune Alliance. The northwestern beach is much narrower than the southeastern beach.

The middle of the island is dominated by Human Impacted Areas with main features such as the lighthouse, the lighthouse keeper building, and the coastguard house. This area is comprised of mostly exotic vegetation such as *Cocos nucifera* and *Dactyloctenium aegyptium*. The interior, north of the lighthouse, is different in composition. There is a large *Opuntia stricta-Hymenocallis latifolia* Dune Alliance polygon to the east of the lighthouse venturing north into a large *Opuntia stricta-Ipomoea alba* Dune Alliance polygon encompassing the majority of the interior north of the lighthouse. The western border north of the lighthouse is also different with mostly Sparse Vegetation-Sand polygons. The northeastern tip of the island has a wide Beach area with an elongated spit of land extending northeast. Some notable communities that were found are the *Conocarpus erectus* Shrubland (ancient climax community), *Cenchrus myosuroides* Dune Association (state-listed graminoid), and *Coccoloba uvifera* Shrubland.

Table 1. Vegetation classes present on Loggerhead Key

Vegetation Class	
Argusia gnaphalodes Scrub	*Hymenocallis latifolia* Dune Association
Argusia gnaphalodes Shrubland	*Ipomoea alba* Dune Association
Argusia gnaphalodes-Suriana maritima Shrubland Alliance	*Iva imbricata-Chamaesyce mesembrianthemifolia-Uniola paniculata* Dune Alliance
Beach	*Melanthera nivea* Dune Association
Cenchrus myosuroides Dune Association	*Opuntia stricta* Dune Association
Chamaesyce mesembrianthemifolia Dune Association	*Opuntia stricta-Hymenocallis latifolia* Dune Alliance
Coccoloba uvifera Shrubland	*Opuntia stricta-Ipomoea alba* Dune Alliance
Conocarpus erectus Shrubland	*Sesuvium portulacastrum* Dune Association
Cordia sebestena Shrubland	Sparse Vegetation-Sand
Cyperus planifolius Dune Association	*Sporobolus virginicus* Dune Association
Eustachys petraea Dune Association	*Suriana maritima* Shrubland
Human Impacted Area	*Uniola paniculata* Dune Association

Bush Key

A total of 206 polygons were created during the October trip. Bush Key has a total of 24 vegetation classes (Table 2, p.15), broken down as follows: 5 Shrubland classes, 3 Scrub classes, 12 Dune classes, 3 Sparse Vegetation classes, and 1 Non-Vegetative class. Bush Key (Figure 3, p. 19 and Appendix B, pp. 93-94) encompasses a 6.44 ha (15.91 acres) area, comprised of 206 polygons. Bush Key has two main parts, a west side and east side, connected by an isthmus or spit of land. Bush Key and Long Key are connected; thus, a boundary was set where the southern beach begins to bend southeast on the east side of Bush Key.

The dominant communities on the western end are mostly comprised of *Cakile lanceolata* Dune Association (0.79 ha) and Mixed Dune Species (0.74 ha). *Cakile lanceolata* Dune Association is common in the interior low dune and on the high outer dune. Similarly, Mixed Dune Species can be found in the same area. Other common communities present west of the isthmus are *Melanthera nivea* Dune Association (0.38 ha), *Portulaca oleracea* Dune Association (0.36 ha), *Sesuvium portulacastrum* Dune Association (0.27 ha), and *Chamaesyce mesembrianthemifolia* Dune Association (0.23 ha). *Melanthera nivea* and *Portulaca oleracea* Dune Associations are found in the low dune of the interior west side. *Sesuvium portulacastrum* Dune Association is also common in the low dune and at or near the edges of the outer dune. Sparse Vegetation-Sand (0.61 ha) is common bordering the north beach (western end), near the isthmus, and the western spit, which extends towards Garden Key. *Chamaesyce mesembrianthemifolia* Dune Association is commonly found in close proximity to the shore usually behind sparse vegetation.

Moving eastward, the isthmus has an *Ipomoea pes-caprae* Dune Association (176 m²) polygon, two small *Argusia gnaphalodes* Scrub polygons (27 m²), Sparse Vegetation-Sand, and the beginning of a long polygon of *Argusia gnaphalodes-Suriana maritima* Shrubland Alliance (597 m²). The east side of Bush Key has a different composition of vegetation from the west side of Bush Key. The dominant communities here are *Chamaesyce mesembrianthemifolia* Dune Association (0.29 ha), *Opuntia stricta* Dune Association (0.20 ha), and *Argusia gnaphalodes* Shrubland (0.14 ha). This side of Bush Key has the only existing community of mangroves on Bush Key. Only one polygon of an *Avicennia germinans-Laguncularia racemosa* Mangrove Shrubland (51 m²) was found and mapped. The dominating feature here is the Coral Rubble (0.83 ha) that dominates the north and east shore of east Bush Key and the south point where Bush Key joins with Long Key. The largest polygon on Bush Key is Beach, which covers 0.87 ha (13.6%) of the island.

Table 2. Vegetation classes present on Bush Key

Vegetation Class	
Argusia gnaphalodes Scrub	*Melanthera nivea* Dune Association
Argusia gnaphalodes Shrubland	Mixed Dune Species
Argusia gnaphalodes-Suriana maritima Shrubland Alliance	*Opuntia stricta* Dune Association
Atriplex pentandra Dune Association	*Portulaca oleracea* Dune Association
Avicennia germinans-Laguncularia racemosa Mangrove Shrubland	Salt Pond
Beach	*Sesuvium portulacastrum* Dune Association
Cakile lanceolata Dune Association	Sparse Vegetation-Sand
Chamaesyce mesembrianthemifolia Dune Association	*Sporobolus domingensis* Dune Association
Coccoloba uvifera Shrubland	*Sporobolus virginicus* Dune Association
Conocarpus erectus Scrub	*Suriana maritima* Scrub
Coral Rubble	*Suriana maritima* Shrubland
Ipomoea pes-caprae Dune Association	*Uniola paniculata* Dune Association

Long Key

Since Long Key is connected to Bush Key, we separated the two islands at the southeastern bend of Bush Key where it starts to thin out and head southward. The total area is 1.09 ha (2.69 acres) (Figure 3, p. 19 and Appendix B, p. 95), comprised of 45 polygons. The island is dominated by mangrove communities with a total of 12 mapping classes (Table 3, p. 16), as follows: 1 Woodland class, 2 Shrubland classes, 4 Scrub classes, 4 Dune classes, and 1 Sparse Vegetation class. Long Key has 4 Mangrove classes found nowhere else in the Dry Tortugas, while the remaining 8 classes can be found on Bush Key and Loggerhead Key. The largest mangrove community is an *Avicennia germinans* Woodland at 0.13 ha (11.5% of the island). The largest vegetative community on Long Key is the *Chamaesyce mesembrianthemifolia* Dune Association (0.18 ha-16.5%). North of the mangroves, the vegetation is stunted with low growing

15

Chamaesyce mesembrianthemifolia (low percent cover) and *Suriana maritima* and *Argusia gnaphalodes* scrubs. This is due to the coral debris substrate which dominates Long Key. A large Coral Rubble polygon covers 0.73 ha (67.3%) of the island. The rest of the island is covered with vegetation over a coral debris substrate. The omnipresent coral debris extends further south of the mangroves but there is little to no vegetation there. The Coral Rubble polygon has less than 5% cover of vegetation.

Table 3. Vegetation classes present on Long Key

Vegetation Class	
Argusia gnaphalodes Scrub	*Ipomoea alba* Dune Association
Argusia gnaphalodes Shrubland	*Laguncularia racemosa* Scrub
Avicennia germinans Shrubland	*Portulaca oleracea* Dune Association
Avicennia germinans Woodland	*Rhizophora mangle* Scrub
Chamaesyce mesembrianthemifolia Dune Association	*Sesuvium portulacastrum* Dune Association
Coral Rubble	*Suriana maritima* Scrub

Garden Key

Garden Key has been heavily influenced over the history of the island. Because of constant human alteration, there is little development of significant native vegetation communities. However, besides the constant fort renovations and foot traffic, there are native vegetation communities which exist on the grounds outside the fort walls. Garden Key is the second largest island at 9 ha (22.24 acres) (Figure 4, p. 20), comprised of 22 polygons. There are a total of 8 vegetation classes (Table 4, p.17) that were identified on Garden Key, as follows: 2 Woodland classes, 1 Shrubland class, 3 Dune classes, 1 Sparse Vegetation class, and 1 Non-Vegetative class. The vegetation on the parade grounds within the fort walls and atop the fort walls was not mapped. The whole fort including the moat wall was categorized as Human Impacted (6.37 ha). Other Human Impacted areas mapped are the north and south coaling docks. Human Impacted areas make up the majority of Garden Key totaling an area of 6.89 ha, which constitutes 77% of the island. The largest vegetation community present is one large *Sporobolus virginicus* Dune Association polygon (1.13 ha). Beach polygons (0.64 ha) were created for the north and southwest beach and the beach extending from the south coaling docks to the north coaling docks. These Beach polygons contain a low percentage of pioneer dune species such as *Cakile lanceolata* and *Chamaesyce mesembrianthemifolia*. Around the campgrounds near the southwestern beach, there are *Conocarpus erectus* Woodlands and one *Coccoloba uvifera* Woodland, while *Coccoloba uvifera* Woodlands and *Conocarpus erectus* Woodlands can be found heading toward the north beach on the east side of Garden Key. The woodland communities found on the eastern side are situated around a brick pile in close proximity to the ongoing renovation efforts. Moreover, this area has been influenced by recent construction machinery which may affect community colonization due to substrate disturbance. Other native communities found on Garden Key are one *Ipomoea pes-caprae* Dune Association and one *Opuntia stricta-Hymenocallis latifolia* Dune Alliance. The only sizable exotic community is *Phoenix dactylifera* near the campgrounds which we categorized as Human Impacted.

16

Table 4. Vegetation classes present on Garden Key

Vegetation Class	
Beach	*Ipomoea pes-caprae* Dune Association
Coccoloba uvifera Shrubland	*Opuntia stricta-Hymenocallis latifolia* Dune Alliance
Coccoloba uvifera Woodland	*Sporobolus virginicus* Dune Association
Conocarpus erectus Woodland	
Human Impacted Area	

Hospital Key

Hospital Key (Figure 5, p. 21) has an area of 0.37 ha (0.91 acres) and is the smallest island in area. Three polygons were created for this island and only one mapping class was used. This island is devoid of plant life, although historically, there has been vegetation present here. This island was visited during the June trip and the only class used to describe the island was Beach. The Beach classification for this island contains solely open sand with no vegetation present. We did find two dune elevations, secondary dune and crown dune, which is why we made a separate polygon for each one (using the same Beach class for both). Hospital Key has a history of movement with seemingly constant shifting sand. For this reason, mapping the different dune elevations may give us some insight into geomorphologic changes of the island.

Middle Key

Middle Key (Figure 6, p. 22) is the second smallest island with an area of 0.39 ha (0.95 acres). It was visited during our June trip. As we did for Hospital Key, three polygons were created with the same mapping class. Similarly, we found no vegetation present on the island; thus, Beach was the only class used to describe Middle Key. The three polygons mark the shoreline, secondary dune, and crown dune. Similarly, this island has had a long history of movement and occasionally is inundated and disappears during the summer.

East Key

The easternmost island in Dry Tortugas National Park, East Key (Figure 7, p. 23) has an area of 2.33 ha (5.75 acres). Fourteen polygons were created for East Key: 5 Beach (1.83 ha) polygons, 1 *Ipomoea pes-caprae* Dune Association (104 m²) polygon, and 8 Sparse Vegetation-Sand (0.49 ha) polygons. The two innermost Beach polygons mark the secondary dune and the crown dune. The majority of the vegetation is growing atop the crown dune, which suggests that this is the most stable part of East Key. The crown dune has sparse *Cakile lanceolata*, *Argusia gnaphalodes*, and *Iva imbricata* scattered throughout. The Sparse Vegetation-Sand communities do not have high enough percent of vegetation coverage to include it as a unique class. The different Sparse Vegetation-Sand polygons illustrated in Figure 7 (p. 23) represent varied cover percentages and species composition. The larger polygon includes very low growing vegetation with a lower percent cover. One polygon was made of an *Ipomoea pes-caprae* Dune Association community.

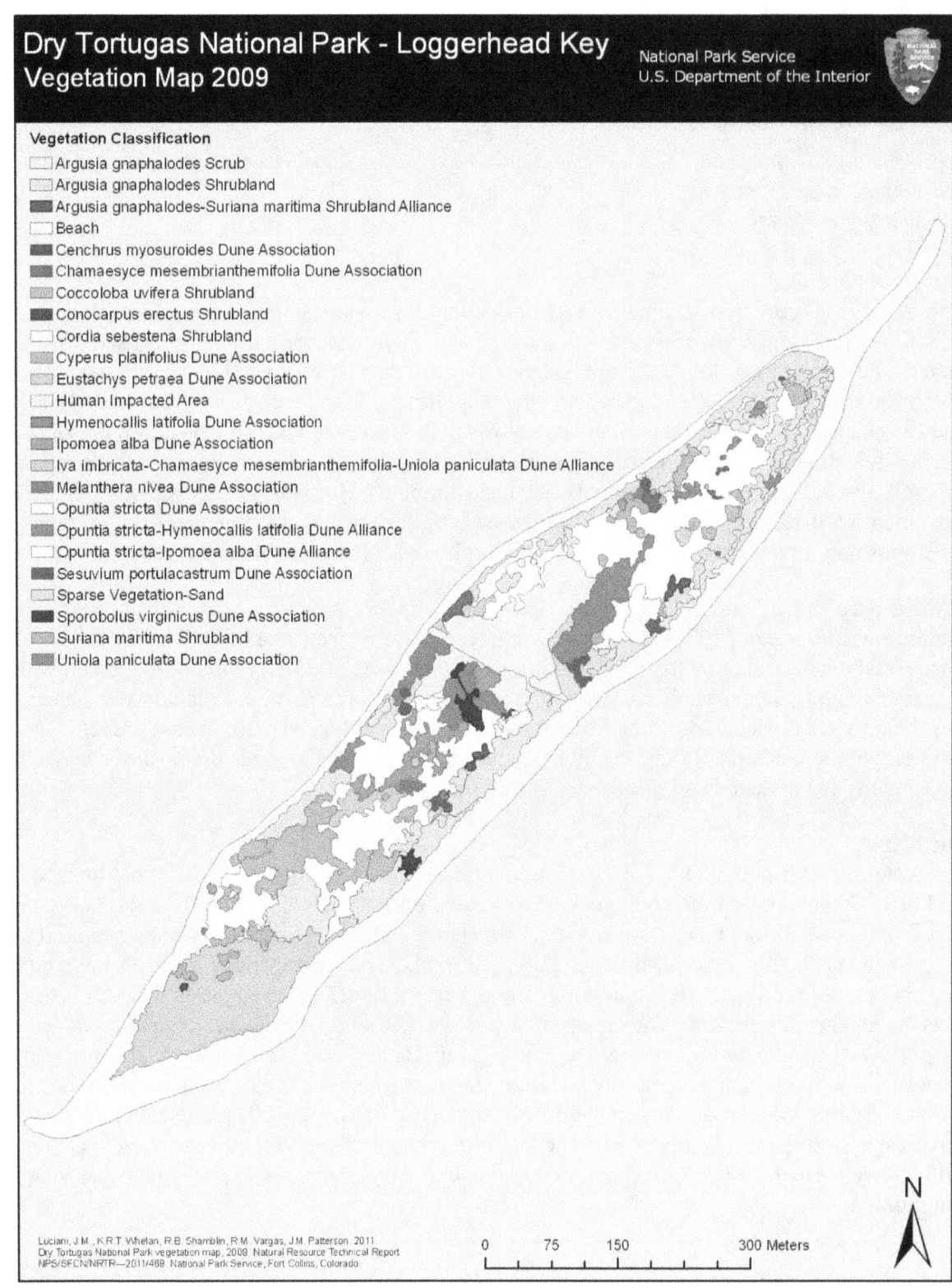

Figure 2. 2009 vegetation map of Loggerhead Key

18

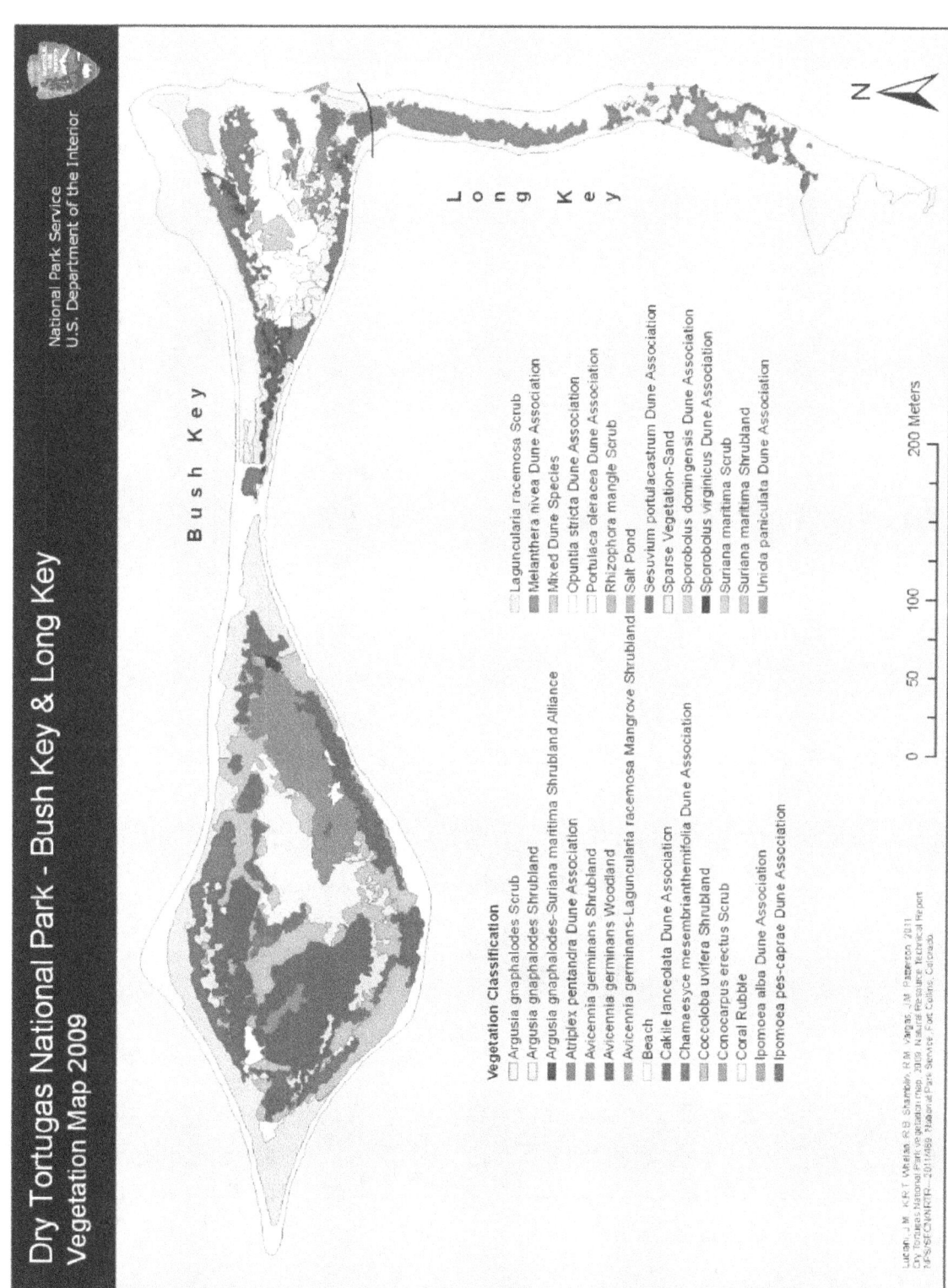

Figure 3. 2009 vegetation map of Bush Key and Long Key

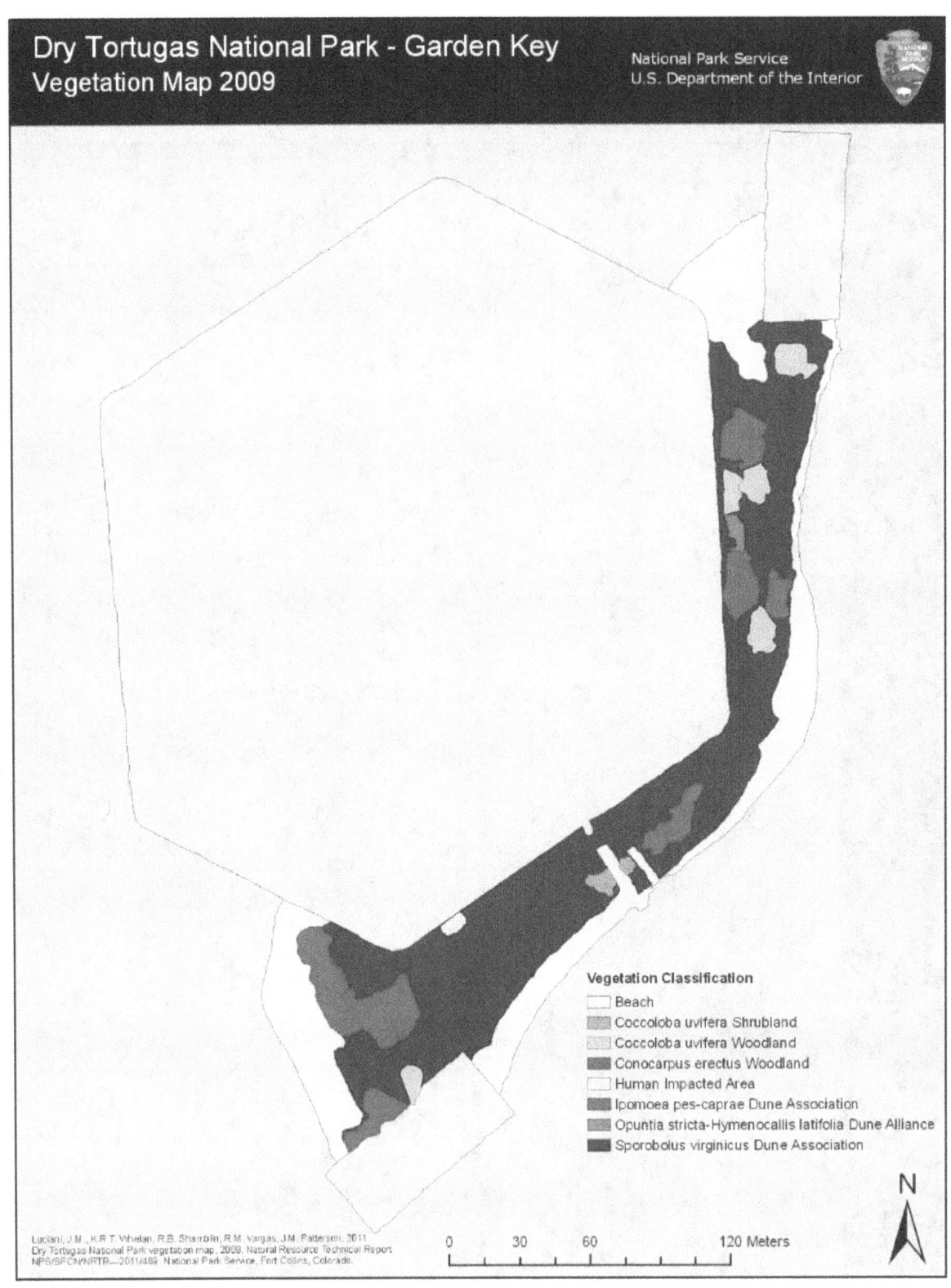

Figure 4. 2009 vegetation map of Garden Key

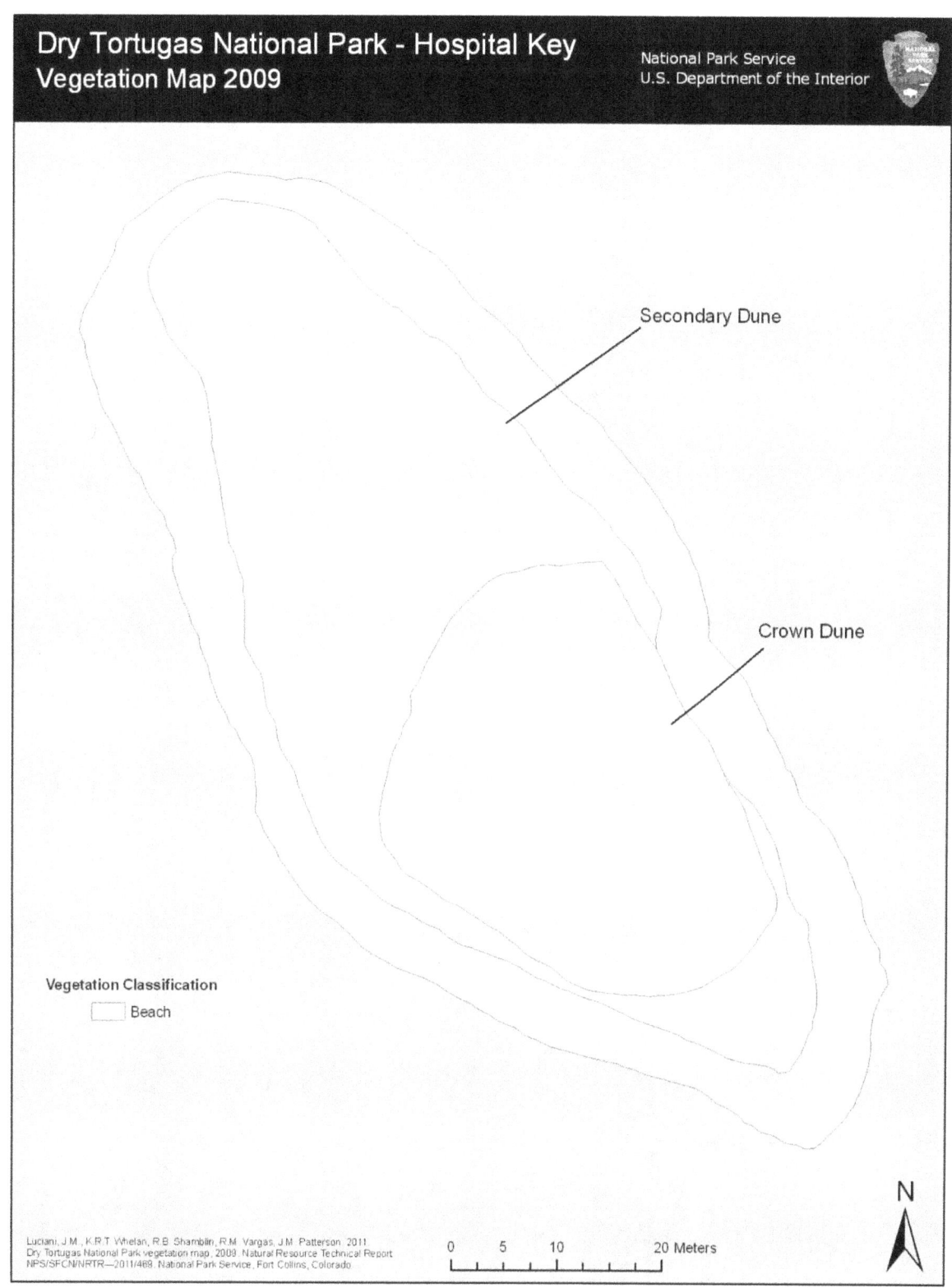

Figure 5. 2009 vegetation map of Hospital Key

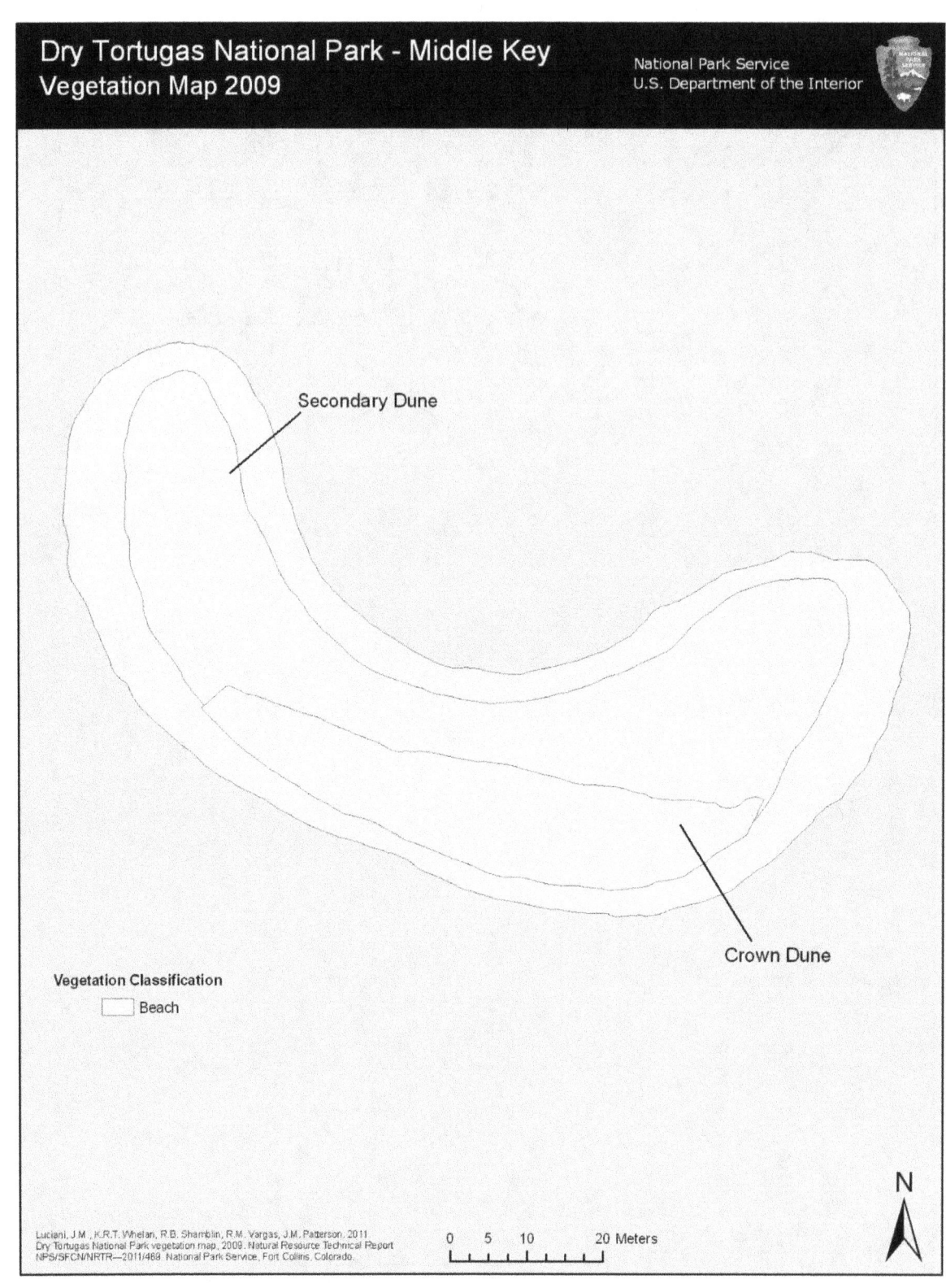

Figure 6. 2009 vegetation map of Middle Key

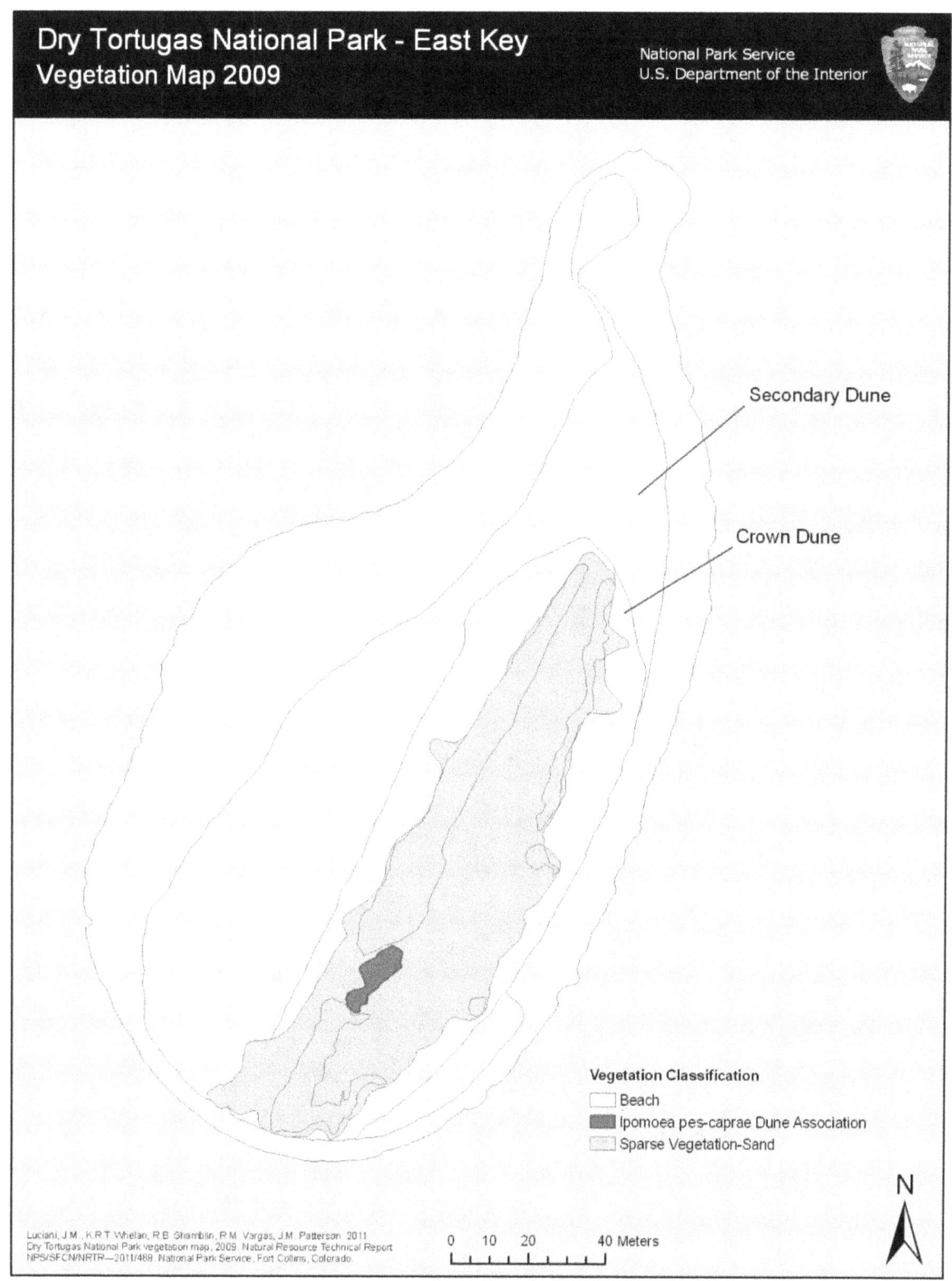

Figure 7. 2009 vegetation map of East Key

Discussion

The Dry Tortugas vegetation map coordinate system is Universal Transverse Mercator zone 17 North, North American Datum of 1983 coordinates with a minimum mapping unit of 25 m². Photointerpretation of aerial imagery was not the method used for the creation of this map. Instead, the mapping was accomplished by using a GPS device to delineate polygons of vegetation communities on the seven islands. This method generates a well-defined map with a small minimum mapping unit. However, this does take time and effort to accomplish. With the bigger and more diverse islands of Loggerhead Key and Bush Key, it took two days to complete mapping each of the islands using the GeoXT GPS unit. Garden Key took more than a half day to finish mapping. Long Key, Hospital Key, Middle Key, and East Key, however, were mapped in a matter of hours. We found two teams of two reduced the time needed for Loggerhead Key and Bush Key. The remaining islands only needed one team of two to accomplish.

The vegetation map has potential to be used in bird and turtle research. The vegetation map can tell which community the migratory birds are inclined to nest in. Meanwhile, the shoreline shapefile can be used to show historical and future turtle nesting sites. Another use for this map is the comparison of historical and future changes of the islands and their vegetation communities. Due to more than a century of marine and terrestrial scientific research, we have the opportunity to examine historical and current communities present on these islands. Besides written descriptions of the vegetation, some historical reports have vegetation maps of several of the islands. The well known historical vegetation maps are from 1904, 1915-16, 1937-38, 1977, and 1993 (Stoddart and Fosberg 1981). Additionally, many aerial images and outlines of the islands have been made for non-floral focused reports. Finally, brief or lengthy accounts of the vegetation on the islands span about a century and a half. Here we will explore the historical and present dominant vegetation communities found on the seven islands. It should be noted that even though botanical studies on these islands span over 100 years, this is a short period compared to the long-term geologic processes that are shaping these islands. Case in point, during his 1773-75 surveys, George Gauld witnessed 11 total islands and now only 7 remain.

Loggerhead Key

Loggerhead Key has had significant vegetation composition changes since the middle part of the 19th century. According to Bowman (1918), there was once "a large stand of old white buttonwood trees, *Conocarpus erectus L.*" Climax communities can be hard to determine due to reoccurring disturbances which prevent the island's peak progression. However, if this evidence is true of a dominant *Conocarpus* community, then their apparent removal could have caused a shift in the island's vegetation morphology. Stoddart and Fosberg (1981) and Bowman (1918) stated that these "old sylvan flora" were "cut down or burned by the residents," mainly by fisherman, circa 1840. Evidently, since then, *Suriana* became the dominating flora on Loggerhead Key. In 1904, E.O. Lansing reported that the sub-climax community of *Suriana maritima* Shrubland dominated the landscape (Millspaugh 1907). The *Suriana* community was still dominant during Bowman's 1915-16 survey on Loggerhead Key. Bowman also noted the ever-increasing presence of an *Opuntia* community existing in the central portions of the island and a *Uniola* community on the northwest corner, eastern shore, and southwestern shore. The *Opuntia* community was then spreading into the cleared portions of the island. Military personnel cleared dense growths of *Suriana* to quarantine victims of the yellow fever epidemics on the island. In addition to human impacts, *Suriana* abundance must undoubtedly have been affected by many hurricanes that have struck the Dry Tortugas in the early 20th century (Figure 8). Bowman recognized how *Casuarina* easily reproduced and seeded, which was introduced by the director of the Carnegie laboratory ca 1910 (Stoddart and Fosberg 1981). Bowman mentioned how flora introductions changed the appearance of the island "by producing shade and conserving water" (Figure 9A, p. 27).

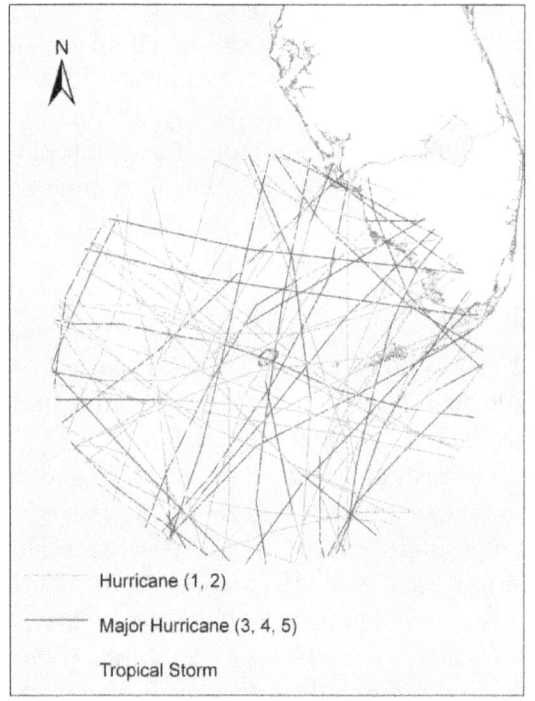 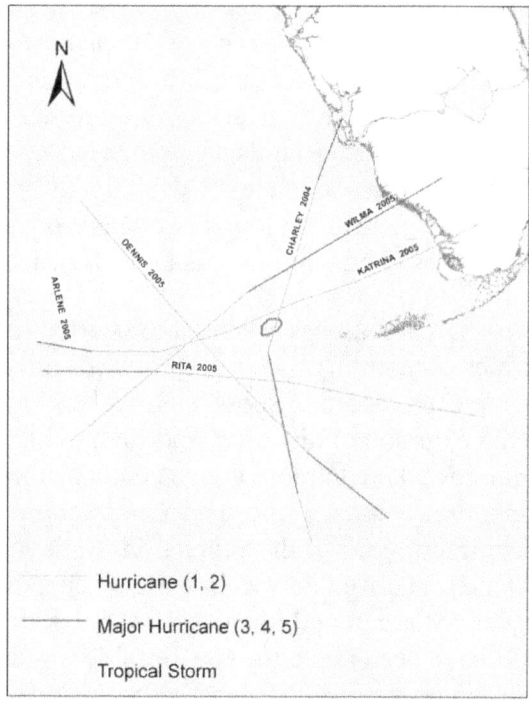

Figure 8. The paths of hurricanes and tropical storms that are within 150 miles of Dry Tortugas National Park. The image on the left contains hurricane tracks from 1851-2008. The image on the right displays hurricanes that impacted Dry Tortugas National Park during the 2004-05 hurricane seasons. The boundary of the park is displayed in dark green.

It wasn't until the 1937-38 surveys of Davis that the dominant *Suriana* consocies were being replaced by "two apparently more xeric plant communities" (Davis 1942). Although still dominant, Davis suggested that the progressive demise of the *Suriana* consocies was due in large part to the size and density of the *Suriana* since "their roots fail[ed] to obtain enough water from the porous soils" (Davis 1942). Thus, this led to more xeric communities, such as *Opuntia,* and the pioneer species *Chamaesyce*. These two species took over bare areas with "certain associated coarse grasses, vines, and plants" (Davis 1942). Davis said *Chamaesyce* grew more abundant in the interior, and Bowman noted that *Chamaesyce* had "not changed position or quantity." However, "*Suriana* still cover[ed] most of the un-cleared parts of the island" (Davis 1942). *Suriana* was losing its dominance on the island. This was evident to the southwest of the lighthouse where only about half of the area consisted of *Suriana*. "In this southwestern part of the island a large part of the area once occupied by *Suriana* [had] been taken over by a growth of *Opuntia, Chamaesyce, Agave americana,* and other plants" (Davis 1942). Davis found *Uniola* dominant in the same areas Bowman had described northeast of the Carnegie laboratory, southwest of the lighthouse, and along the coast on the dune plateau (Davis 1942). Other areas described by Davis are those strand-beach communities growing on the fore dunes and the beach mostly made up of *Sesuvium, Ipomoea, Sporobolus, Uniola, Argusia,* and other pioneer species.

Two exotic invasive species *Agave* and *Casuarina* were becoming more prolific on the island by the time of Davis, in which he predicted their utter dominance on the island (Figure 9B). *Agave decipiens* and *Agave sisalana* spread well since their introduction, due to the dry sandy soils on the island. The success of *Agave* spp. was most likely correlated to the success of *Casuarina* and its nitrogen-fixating ability. *Cocos nucifera* was also quite prominent, being one of the few tree species present on the island at the time, but was restricted to human impacted areas around the lighthouse and the Carnegie Laboratory. Most of the other introductions have not had the burgeoning success the other exotics exhibited. Plantings were not limited to exotics. For instance, both authors wrote how "clearing and encouragement by man have increased the number of *Hymenocallis*" (Davis 1942). *Hymenocallis* grows naturally on the island but was planted as well because of its aesthetic value.

Figure 9. Photos looking northeast from the top of the lighthouse. The top two photos show the path between the Laboratory and the lighthouse. **Figure 9A:** Photo from Bowman (1918). Bowman described that the dark areas were occupied by *Suriana* and lighter ones by *Opuntia* and *Ipomoea* with the Laboratory buildings in the distance. **Figure 9B:** Photo from Davis (1942). Davis described thickets of *Suriana* growing on either side of the path and pointed out the *Cocos nucifera* near the lighthouse and the tall growth of *Casuarina* around the Laboratory building. **Figure 9C:** Photo taken in 1995 from Pernas *et al.* (2001). A tall woodland of *Casuarina* covered the island at that time. **Figure 9D:** Photo taken in 2001 by Tony Pernas after herbicide treatment of Australian pine along with logging and post-burning.

By the time of Stoddart and Fosberg's report in 1981, they described a complete transformation of vegetation. A tall woodland of *Casuarina* was the dominant community on Loggerhead Key and native communities were greatly reduced since Davis. "By 1980, the words of Davis came to fruition, as nearly all of the native communities were displaced and out competed by two species, Australian pine (*Casuarina*) and century plant (*Agave* spp.)" (Figure 9C, p. 27) (Pernas *et al.* 2001). After Dry Tortugas National Park was established in 1992, resource managers began to discuss restoration efforts for Loggerhead Key (NPS 2000). In 1995, a plan was developed to eradicate *Casuarina* and *Agave* spp. due to their destructive alterations to the native plant communities and animals of the island. By 2001, essentially all of the exotic species had been removed on the island (Pernas *et al.* 2001). *Casuarina* had a very damaging effect on the island due to its allelopathic qualities. The understory was quite depleted of native herbs due to a thick layer of leaf litter from the pine needles of *Casuarina*. After the island was treated and burned, vegetation response from restoring the island to pre-Australian pine conditions saw a "concomitant increase in the numbers of native species" (Pernas *et al.* 2001) (Figure 9D, p. 27). An important fact to mention is the nitrogen fixating property of *Casuarina*: after removing the exotics, available soil nitrogen may have played a role in the island's initial response to restoration, since there is otherwise commonly poor nutrient availability in the system.

Figure 10. Vegetation succession since after the 2005 hurricane season. **Figure 10A:** Photo taken by Tony Pernas. Northeast end of Loggerhead Key in 2006, after the 2005 hurricane season. **Figure 10B:** Photo taken by Jose Luciani. The conditions of Loggerhead Key during the 2009 vegetation mapping effort. In the photo is a large community of *Opuntia stricta-Hymenocallis latifolia* just east of the building. Circular bushes are mostly shrubs of *Argusia* and *Suriana*. The middle interior is mostly *Opuntia stricta-Ipomoea alba*.

Since the island was cleared of exotics, native dominated communities have re-established. The clearing allowed succulents and herbs to dominate the landscape. Specifically, *Opuntia stricta* probably played a large role in re-colonizing the treated areas, which most likely had drier soils due to prescribed fire and open landscape. Pioneer species also had success re-colonizing the island. In general, vines, grasses and succulents were the dominant vegetation post-restoration. The shrubs, *Argusia* and *Suriana*, took many years to re-establish and have yet to proliferate like in past years. Hurricanes in 2004 and 2005 prevented vegetative succession. The more significant hurricanes hindered years of community progress (Figure 10A). However, this is natural in the Dry Tortugas and allows new communities to rise up. Today, Loggerhead Key is still recovering from restoration and hurricanes (Figure 10B). The once dominant *Suriana* community now has a total area of 1.26 ha, which is only 6.4% of the island's total area of 19.75 ha. *Argusia gnaphalodes* Shrubland is becoming the dominant shrub on the island instead of *Suriana*. At 2.23 ha, *Argusia* constitutes 11.3% of the island being most prominent on the dune plateaus surrounding the interior vegetation and in some interior places south and north of the lighthouse. In most cases, *Argusia* grows next or near *Suriana* patches. The two species also grow intermixed which may indicate competition between the two dominant shrubs. *Argusia* appears to be outcompeting *Suriana* under current conditions, since restoration and hurricane disturbance. Other shrubland communities found on the island are *Coccoloba uvifera* Shrubland (0.3%), *Conocarpus erectus* Shrubland (0.03%), and *Cordia sebestena* Shrubland (1.2%).

In fact, the common vegetation found is a mixture of graminoids, succulents, and herbaceous plants. The total of the three vegetation types make up 38.4% of the island. Within this percentage, *Opuntia stricta-Ipomoea alba* Dune Alliance (12.1%), *Iva imbricata-Chamaesyce mesembrianthemifolia-Uniola paniculata* Dune Alliance (9.1%), *Opuntia stricta* Dune Association (6.9%), and *Opuntia stricta-Hymenocallis latifolia* (3.7%) comprise the most of that percentage. *Opuntia* is found in three of the four above mentioned communities. This exemplifies the dominance of *Opuntia* in the interior spaces of the island.

Bush Key

Bush Key has grown in size since 1904 when Lansing and Millspaugh excluded this island from the survey and report because, according to Millspaugh (1907), it was "so low as to be awash during heavy weather and, on this account, [was] void of vegetation." Vegetation records began with Bowman (1918). His account of the vegetation is brief and unclear. The orientation and topography of the vegetation map done by Bowman seemed to be off by 90° and inaccurate according to Davis (1942). Bowman stated "the flora of the island [was] quite varied and well scattered." He did mention the presence of 12-year-old *Suriana* and *Argusia* plants that Lansing overlooked in his account of the island in 1904. Young *Rhizophora* seedlings grew on the south shore of Bush Key (Figure 11, p. 30) and a clump of three to four-year-old mangroves grew around landlocked tidal pools (Bowman 1918). The landlocked pools were caused from dredging of Bush Key in 1901-05 to be used for fill on Garden Key (Stoddart and Fosberg 1981). The *Rhizophora* plants could have rooted from human intervention but were most likely distributed from two *Rhizophora* individuals, "about 2 meters tall, which had flowers and fruits in 1916" (Bowman 1918) that were growing on the edge of the eastern coaling docks on Garden Key. Bowman described the distribution of species present on Bush Key but failed to describe or display the communities. Many of the species Bowman displayed on his map (Appendix C, p. 101) can still be seen today on Bush Key.

29

Figure 11. *Rhizophora* seedlings on the beach of Bush Key as described by Bowman. Photo from Bowman (1918).

The island size and shape increased and changed by the time Davis did his surveys. Davis posed the first reliable vegetation map of Bush Key. Since Bowman, the two sand ridges, as shown in his map, joined and began extending westward and eastward. Davis also described that Bush Key had "very mixed vegetation" (Figure 12A). At that time, there were few distinct communities consisting of small groups of similar vegetation and many scattered individuals. Davis described there were few patches of *Suriana* and *Opuntia* with the former more widespread than the latter. The most common communities consisted individually of *Chamaesyce*, *Uniola*, *Sesuvium*, and *Argusia*. The interior had three ponds. One of the ponds had a *Laguncularia* association with a few *Rhizophora* plants (Davis 1942). *Rhizophora* was also planted around another pond. The last pond had a thicket of buttonwoods (Davis 1942). There is uncertainty in how the mangrove species got to the most isolated part of the Florida Keys, but by the time of Davis all four mangrove species had rooted on Bush Key. The rest of the island eastward was largely made up of coral debris and scattered communities such as *Chamaesyce*.

Figure 12. Historic and current images of Bush Key. **Figure12A:** Photo from Davis (1942). **Figure 12B:** Photo taken by SFCN of the conditions of Bush Key during the 2009 vegetation mapping effort.

A fire occurred on Bush Key late in 1942 from an unidentified aircraft bombing the island, according to Robertson (1964). This fire burned all the vegetation. By 1946, Sprunt described a "remarkable spread of vegetation on Bush Key" (Robertson 1964). *Laguncularia* and *Rhizophora* were still present around the ponds with large areas of the island covered by *Salicornia* and *Argusia* (Stoddart and Fosberg 1981). In 1962, Fosberg found similar vegetation covering the ponds with much of the island covered by 2 m tall *Suriana* and by *Opuntia* with scattered *Uniola, Sporobolus*, and *Sesuvium* (Stoddart and Fosberg 1981). By the time of the

1981 vegetation map of Stoddart and Fosberg, Bush Key had narrowed from erosion along both northern and southern shores (Stoddart and Fosberg 1981). There were thickets of both *Conocarpus* and *Laguncularia* and a developing *Avicennia* woodland on the eastern spit. This spit had scattered vegetation such as *Suriana, Argusia, Sesuvium, Cakile, Chamaesyce,* and *Ipomoea*. On the main part of the island, west of the spit, there was a large community of tall grasses accompanied by lesser communities of *Sesuvium, Suriana,* and a mixed community of *Cakile, Sesuvium, Chamaesyce,* and *Ipomoea*. Scattered communities of *Argusia* and *Opuntia* were throughout the island west of the spit. *Casuarina* was first recorded in 1977 and removed around 1998-99. The exotic community never developed here as it did on Loggerhead Key.

Over the years after 1977, Bush Key grew in all directions. By 2009, the eastern spit widened while the larger western end of the island widened on the southern and northern shore (Figure 12B, p. 30). The jut of sand on the western shore lengthened towards Garden Key and in some years, both islands were connected. Similarly, coral fragments eventually piled up to join Bush Key and Long Key. The historic eastern spit became an isthmus that now connects the west side and east side of Bush Key. According to Doyle *et al.* (2002), Davis's (1940) mangrove population was destroyed and the most recently emerged mangroves date back to after Davis (1940). Reimus and Robertson (2001) found an *Avicennia germinans* grove and a few *Rhizophora mangle* seedlings on the east end of the key and some *Laguncularia racemosa* being eroded on the north shore. But the once healthy stand of mangrove species was gradually changing. The *Laguncularia* and *Conocarpus* died off from erosion due to heavy storms and hurricanes (Figure 13A). The existing *Conocarpus* community succumbed to an increased concentration of nutrients from pelican guano which covered the leaves causing a loss of chlorophyll (Doyle *et al.* 2002). The *Avicennia* woodland shrank to a small community of *Avicennia-Laguncularia* woodland (51 m²) southwest of the historic mangrove community along the eroded eastern shoreline. When the island was revisited in May 2010, this community had died off from erosion (Figure 13B). As of May 2010, Bush Key contained no more mangrove association –this community is in the current vegetation map for historic context.

Figure 13. Hurricane and erosion damage on Bush Key. **Figure 13A:** Aerial image of Bush Key after Hurricane Wilma in 2005. The island was partly denuded of vegetation and the mangroves suffered greatly. **Figure 13B:** Photo by Jose Luciani of the eastern shoreline of Bush Key in May 2010. This area used to have a mangrove woodland, but erosion and storms have claimed the presence of mangroves.

Like years past, Bush Key is an island of mixed vegetation. In October 2009, the island was 6.44 ha (15.9 acres) and was defined by a mix of herbaceous and succulent plants. The common dune communities consisted of *Cakile lanceolata* Dune Association (12.2%), Low Dune Species

(11.4%), *Chamaesyce mesembrianthemifolia* Dune Association (8.1%), *Melanthera nivea* Dune Association (6.5%), *Portulaca oleracea* Dune Association (5.9%), *Sesuvium portulacastrum* Dune Association (5.1%), and *Opuntia stricta* Dune Association (3.6%). The community, Low Dune Species, contained many scattered intermixed dune species with undefined dominance. *Cakile*, Low Dune, *Melanthera*, and *Portulaca* communities were more commonly found on the west side of Bush Key. *Chamaesyce* was commonly found on both sides along the dune plateaus. *Opuntia* was common in the interior east side and less so on the west side. Small communities of *Melanthera*, *Portulaca*, and *Sesuvium* can be found along the southern shore on the east side and on the coral fragments close to the eastern shore. Shrub communities are significantly less than on Loggerhead, the largest being *Argusia gnaphalodes* Shrubland (4.4%). A mixed community of *Argusia-Suriana* (1.3%) and a community of *Suriana* (0.8%) have a smaller percentage of total area when compared to the entire island.

Long Key

This is an island made up mostly of coral debris. Over time, coral debris piled up to form Long Key as it is today. Strong waves helped develop this island extend northward, eventually joining it to Bush Key, and southward. The island was awash and without vegetation when Lansing surveyed it in 1904 (Stoddart and Fosberg 1981). Bowman's illustration of Long Key is difficult to interpret because of the incorrect orientation of the map according to Davis (1942). After Bowman, Long Key was simply a coral ridge with scattered vegetation lacking in mangrove associations. Significant vegetation began growing on the island by the time of Davis's mangrove dispersal experiments. *Rhizophora* seedlings were able to root between low-tide and high-tide levels (Davis 1942). Davis also planted many *Rhizophora* seedlings with differing tidal flux depths. Many of these seedlings survived over the years. Other mangrove associations were promoted by the presence of *Rhizophora*. *Avicennia* was present in small numbers on the higher elevations of the coral island. *Avicennia* was not planted by Davis, but was present on Bush Key. Lastly, small communities of *Salicornia*, *Sesuvium*, and *Batis* made up the herb layer on the intermediate to higher elevations of the island (Davis 1942).

Figure 14. Mangroves on Long Key in 2005 and 2010. **Figure 14A:** Aerial image of Long Key after Hurricane Wilma in 2005. **Figure 14B:** Photo by Jose Luciani of current mangrove conditions, May 2010.

The mangroves continued to grow over the years. "In 1977 Stoddart found a woodland of *Rhizophora* and *Avicennia* 4.5 m tall on the west side of the beach ridge, with strand shrubs and herbs on the seaward side" (Stoddart and Fosberg). The mangroves thrived to a point in which the community was a thick forest supporting nesting and roosting habitat for magnificent

32

frigatebirds and brown noddys. The frigatebirds created suitable growing conditions for vegetation by providing nutrients in otherwise inhospitable condition, because coral substrate is lacking in organic matter (Doyle *et al*. 2002). "The added nutrients improve mangrove photosynthesis and water-use efficiency, resulting in enhanced growth" (Doyle *et al*. 2002). However, "excessive nutrient loading can cause overgrowth stress and kill them" (Doyle *et al*. 2002). In 2005, hurricanes battered the mangroves to such a degree that it is unlikely they will recover to their former extent (Figure 14A, p. 32). In 2009, the mangroves are still recovering (Figure 14B, p. 32). There were four communities of mangroves. *Avicennia germinans* Woodland (1,254 m²) is the dominant vegetation feature, with small patches of *Avicennia germinans* Shrubland (92 m²), *Laguncularia racemosa* Scrub (24 m²), and *Rhizophora mangle* Scrub (11 m²). The coral ridge north of the mangroves consists mostly of *Chamaesyce mesembrianthemifolia* Dune Association (16.5%) with interspersed *Suriana* and *Argusia* individuals. Within the mangroves, small patches of *Chamaesyce*, *Argusia*, *Ipomoea*, and *Portulaca* exist atop the thick coral rubble. Most of the island is composed of coral rubble, which seems to be accumulating.

Garden Key
The original island is thought to once have had a remnant of *Conocarpus* forest or thickets. Bowman described a grove of old *Conocarpus* trees within the parade grounds of the fort. These untouched *Conocarpus* trees must have been an important feature of the historical landscape on Garden Key. The construction of Fort Jefferson led to an influx of plant introductions. Consequently, native communities were lost during the construction. Outside the fort walls, the small areas of sand have been so disturbed throughout the years during the fort's building and occupancy, that the vegetation is less significant than in other islands (Davis 1942). The focus of native vegetation in this report is on the communities outside the fort walls, as this is where they can develop under some degree of a natural environment. As for the plants within fort walls, Bowman put it best: they have "been too much under artificial influence to be of much importance in an ecological study." Millspaugh and Bowman described species distribution outside the fort walls very well (Appendix C, p. 98 and p. 100). Both Millspaugh and Bowman explained that the larger southern side on the exterior grounds of the fort had a larger number of species, both native and exotic, than the northern strip mostly due to human occupancy and transportation of commodities from the southern dock to the sally-port. In Millspaugh's report, the exterior fort grounds had two sections: a northeast and southern sand area. Along the west beach of the southern sand area, communities consisted of a "stretch of *Paspalum vaginatum*," a "complete border of *Uniola* with a fringe of *Cenchrus tribuloides*," patches of *Cyperus*, and *Canavalia rosea* "separated from the *Uniola* by a growth of *Chamaesyce*" (Millspaugh 1907). The southern interior contained a heterogeneous mixture of *Ipomoea pes-caprae*, *Chamaesyce*, *Atriplex*, *Suriana*, *Argusia*, *Portulaca*, *Canavalia*, *Eustachys*, *Melanthera*, and *Heliotropium curassavicum*, among others (Millspaugh 1907). The northeast sand area contained a mixture of *Paspalum vaginatum*, *Cakile*, *Sesuvium*, *Uniola*, *Argusia*, *Suriana*, *Chamaesyce*, *Cenchrus echinatus*, and *Iva* with an eastern border of *Cenchrus tribuloides* and *Cyperus* (Millspaugh 1907).

Over a decade later, the vegetation stretching the western sand ridge was composed of a "thick association of *Uniola* interspersed with *Conyza*, *Cenchrus*, *Iva*, and *Canavalia*," associations of *Argusia* and *Opuntia*, and smaller associations of *Ipomoea pes-caprae* and *Stachytarpheta*

(Bowman 1918). There were numerous grasses with the fairly abundant *Sporobolus* and some *Cyperus* located west of the walk leading to the sally-port (Bowman 1918). The area south of the southeast corner of the fort had relative abundances of *Alternanthera maritima*, *Sesuvium*, *Stachytarpheta*, and *Hymenocallis* (Bowman 1918). The northern strip east of the fort was composed of *Sesbania vesicaria*, *Argusia*, *Ipomoea pes-caprae*, *Canavalia*, *Sporobolus*, *Scaevola*, *Suriana*, *Chamaesyce*, *Uniola*, and *Iva* with some *Ipomoea violacea* and *Cakile* (Bowman 1918).

Davis found four distinct plant communities. A *Uniola* association was the largest, existing mainly on the southwestern part of the island, as well as east of the fort. *Suriana* groups were growing east of the fort, and *Sesuvium* consocies were common east of the fort leading up to the north coaling docks. Lastly, a modified *Chamaesyce* community was found on the southwest sand area with many weed species (Davis 1942). There was also a large lawn area which can still be found today. Davis lumped many species into these common associations, whereas, both Millspaugh and Bowman gave a clear representation of species present on Garden Key. Stoddart and Fosberg did not map Garden Key, and their report lacks any description of the vegetation therein at that time.

The 2005 hurricane season had serious impacts on the fort and vegetation. Heavy erosion and over wash changed the shape of the island and the vegetation was at risk of mortality. Garden Key was mapped in June 2009, and later in May 2010 (to complete mapping the human impacted areas and the shoreline). The central vegetation features are the *Conocarpus erectus* Woodland (2.5%) and the *Coccoloba uvifera* Woodland (0.8%), although not as widespread as the lawn grass, *Sporobolus virginicus* (12.5%). Other native growing communities on Garden Key are *Ipomoea pes-caprae* Dune Association, *Opuntia stricta-Hymenocallis latifolia* Dune Alliance, and sparse pioneer species along the beach.

East Key
This is the largest of the three islands extending northeast from Garden Key. The stability of East Key has led to a history of consistent vegetation data since 1904 when reliable vegetation records began. The vegetation has mostly stayed the same over the years with a low diversity of pioneer dune species. Since this is the most outlying island, "the ecologic influences governing the distribution of the species have been undisturbed" (Bowman 1918). Bowman showed eight species present on East Key with fairly thick growths of *Cenchrus*, *Chamaesyce*, *Cakile*, and *Uniola*. *Argusia* had "large, well-grown bushes" with smaller patches of *Iva* and *Scaevola*. Bowman stated that in "12 years gone by all the species ha[d] held their footing and some ha[d] increased in amount." He stated that since Lansing's 1904 survey the vegetation had stayed the same. During surveys done by Davis in the late 1930s, *Suriana* was beginning to form on the dune plateau. This indicates the steady topography of the island because *Suriana* needs a stable environment to develop, and Davis said the island had "become more stabilized in the past half-century." He described that much of the vegetation consisted of a *Uniola* association with other strand beach plants such as *Ipomoea*, *Sesuvium*, and *Cenchrus*. In 1946 Sprunt found principal growths of *Uniola*, *Argusia*, and *Suriana* with a good amount of *Ipomoea pes-caprae* (Stoddart and Fosberg 1981). Robertson (1964) reported "sizeable bushes" of *Suriana*, *Argusia*, and *Scaevola*. In 1977 Stoddart and Fosberg described an island dominated by an open *Uniola* community with scattered groups of *Scaevola*, *Suriana*, *Argusia*, *Cakile*, *Iva*, and *Sesuvium*.

As of 2009, East Key is the fourth largest island with a total area of 2.33 ha. The island was then dominated by sparse vegetation of *Cakile* and *Chamaesyce* with scattered bushes of *Iva* and *Argusia* seedlings. A well-defined community of Ipomoea pes-caprae was the only sizable community present on the island in 2009. As of 2010, *Chamaesyce* has spread out with more mature and fairly distributed scrubs of *Argusia* and *Iva*. The *Ipomoea* community has grown in size covering more area. However, the majority of the island is still covered with sparse vegetation of *Cakile* and *Chamaesyce*. The shape and area of the island has also changed with a wider eastern beach. East Key is not excluded from changes in position. The island has a long history of movement and changing island size (Figure 15). In 1979 a "change in morphology which [was] related to seasonal changes in predominant wind direction" was described by Davis and O'Neill.

Middle Key and Hospital Key

These two islands have had a varied topographic history and their location has consistently shifted due to oceanic processes (Figure 15). Shifting sands, salt water inundation, and blistering sands limits the amount of vegetation that can grow on these two islands. Bowman noted dead *Cakile* tufts on Middle Key and several dead *Cakile* and individual *Scaevola* and *Iva* plants on Hospital Key. Davis only recorded a few individuals of *Cakile*, *Iva*, and *Chamaesyce* on Middle Key, whereas Hospital Key supported *Uniola*, *Argusia*, and *Chamaesyce* (Davis 1942). In 1977, both islands were devoid of vegetation. As of 2009, Hospital Key and Middle Key have no vegetation on it. Middle Key is the larger of the two islands with a crescent shape to it.

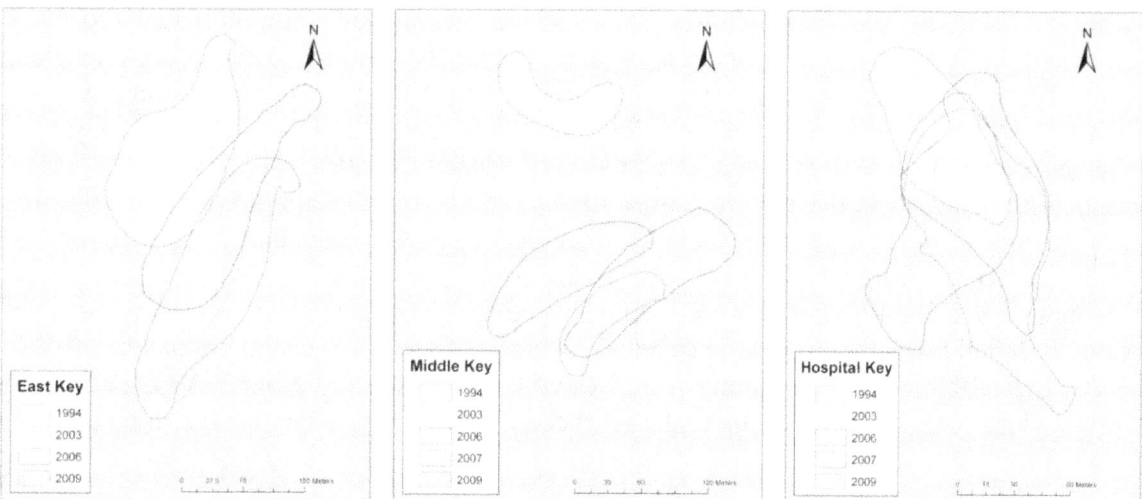

Figure 15. Historic shoreline changes for East Key, Middle Key, and Hospital Key

2009 Vegetation Map Compared to Vegetation Transects on Loggerhead Key

Vegetation transects were established on Loggerhead Key in 1994 to monitor the recovery of native vegetation during the treatment and removal of the introduced *Casuarina* and *Agave*. During 1994-2001, ten transects were sampled annually to monitor the recovery success of native vegetation under management activities (Pernas *et al.* 2001). The yearly sampling data showed a reduction in exotic species in the managed areas with an increase of native species (Pernas *et al.* 2001). Eventually, all the exotic species were removed by 2001 (Pernas *et al.* 2001). Vegetation monitoring by transects was resumed in 2004 to not only continue restoration monitoring, but to also monitor general vegetation changes after the 2004 and 2005 hurricane season (Sadle 2007). The line-intercept sampling method was continued, to be consistent with Pernas *et al.* (2001). From 2004-2009, a subset of vegetation transects were sampled, mainly due to inability to relocate transect marking posts. During the 2009 sample survey, marking posts were secured with the installation of 8 ft long, 9/16 inch thick stainless steel survey rods (buried 5 ft into the sediment) with an identification tag attached. Transects ran the width of the island from northwest to southeast. Each transect was broken into 25 m subsections. Figure 16 (p. 37) displays the location of the vegetation transects that were sampled in 2009. The figure shows that the northwest tip of transect 7 was been lost to beach erosion.

The mapping effort and the transect survey occurred at the same time, so we have the unique opportunity to compare how the transects represent the vegetation communities of the island. To compare the results from the transect data and the vegetation map, the relative abundance of species encountered during the sampling by line-intercept of each transect was compared with the relative abundance of the community types present on the current Loggerhead Key vegetation map. We excluded Beach, Sparse Vegetation-Sand, and Human Impacted Areas present on the map because these areas were not covered by the transects. Thus, the total map area consists only of species-specific communities that can correlate easily in the comparison. Table 12 (p. 50) compares the relative abundance of all the species encountered along all five transects and the community classes from the vegetation map for the entire island. Table 13 (pp. 51-52) compares the relative abundance of species found only on the transect or only on the vegetation map for each of the five transects. Some of the species encountered along the transects were rare and did not form a large enough patch to be named as a community and are therefore not listed on the vegetation map. Also, some of the mapped community types form alliances consisting of two or three species grouped into one community. This prevents the data from directly matching up, but meaningful comparisons can still be made. The vegetation transect data shows that the combination of *Ipomoea alba* (22.95%), *Opuntia stricta* (20.71%), and *Hymenocallis latifolia* (0.58%) has a relative abundance of 44.24% which is similar to the corresponding alliances on the map that cover 42.49% of the island. Among the comparable species, there is a general agreement for 80% to 90% of the relative abundance between the two methods. The species with a higher frequency of occurrence along the transects are more likely to have their own community or be a co-dominant species. The vegetation transect data tells us more about the relative abundance of individual species, whereas the vegetation map lacks this detail due to the defining of community types by the dominant species. Nonetheless, the transects as a whole characterize the vegetation on Loggerhead Key well when compared to the vegetation map.

Table 13 (pp. 51-52) breaks down the comparison by transect. In order to achieve comparable measures, the relative abundance of community classes was calculated by summing the linear distance along each individual transect for each community class intersected by the transect then dividing each by the total distance. Also, the relative abundance of species for the individual transects was calculated by summing the total distance of each species on the transect divided by the distance covered by vegetation. For transects 1 and 4, the individual transect data does not compare well to the vegetation communities on the map. However, transects 7, 11, and 12 have a more favorable comparison. These results show that non-patchy species make up a significant portion of the transect and are not represented in the vegetation map. This affects the direct comparability of the vegetation communities to the transect data because the community class definition masks the inherent species richness of the community. So, just as future vegetation maps of the Dry Tortugas are necessary to document changes in vegetation communities, annual vegetation transect sampling on Loggerhead Key are crucial to monitor vegetation status such as individual species abundance, diversity, and exotic invasion.

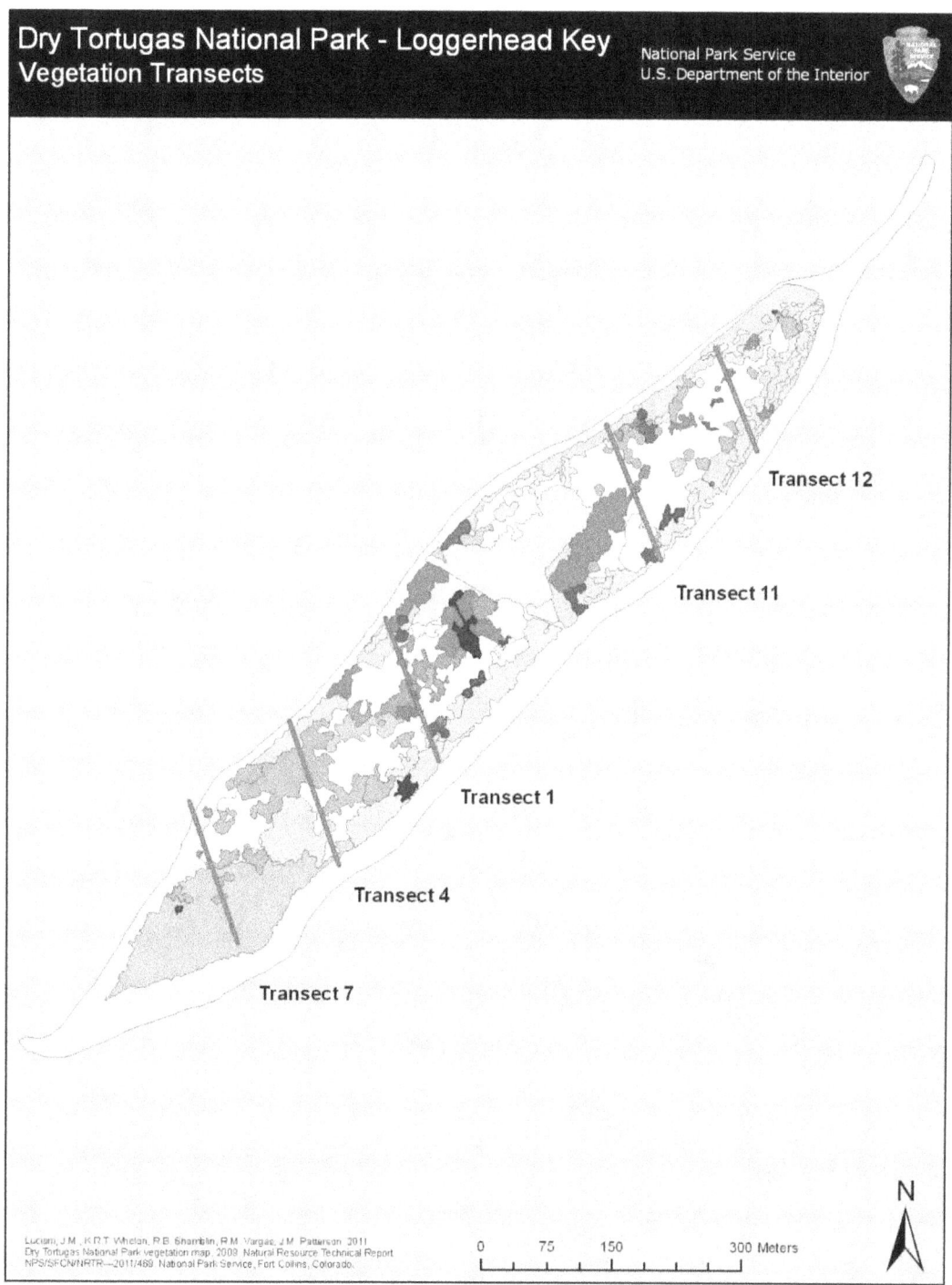

Figure 16. The location of transects sampled in 2009

Conclusion

The 2009 Dry Tortugas Vegetation Map was created using in-field delineation of each map polygon using the Trimble GeoXT. This method generated a vegetation map that is finely detailed with a small minimum mapping unit (25 m²). Although the Dry Tortugas has a rich history in vegetation mapping, never has it been accomplished at such a fine scale of detail. The polygon delineation occurred in the field with full visitation (vegetation census) of the entire area, so the classification and map accuracy is assumed to be extremely high and, although not independently tested, we feel it easily meets the National Vegetation Inventory Program standard of 80% classification accuracy with 90% confidence. Table 14 (p. 53) summarizes the products and filenames included in the Dry Tortugas National Park vegetation mapping project DVD.

During the 2009 Dry Tortugas Vegetation Map project we were able to document very specific definitions for the 41 vegetation map classes present on the seven islands. This is a modernization and improvement from the last defining work which was Davis's 1942 description representing the first community-driven vegetation map of the Dry Tortugas, whereas his predecessors focused more on species distribution and species diversity. However, limitations caused Davis to lump a number of the smaller vegetation communities together, and here we are able to delineate, to a smaller scale, patch size associations. The vegetation mapping project documents the current vegetation communities present on the seven islands in a spatially relevant matter. This new product is useful to help explore a number of current resource management issues. One such issue is habitat use associations of a number of nesting bird species present on the islands like the sooty tern, brown noddy, magnificent frigatebird, bridled tern, masked booby, and the threatened roseate tern. This map can also help identify available nesting beach area for endangered green and loggerhead sea turtles. This product is useful for the identification of habitat and location of listed Florida plant species such as the big sandbur, sea lavender, erect pricklypear, and inkberry. Along with the above uses, this vegetation map provides a clear and concise snapshot of the vegetation communities present in the Dry Tortugas.

Table 5. Additional description of community types – South Florida / Dry Tortugas formations

Vegetation Physiognomic Class	South Florida/Dry Tortugas Formation
Woodland	Mangrove Woodland
	Upland Woodland
Shrubland	Mangrove Shrubland
	Upland Shrubland
Scrub	Mangrove Scrub
	Upland Scrub
Dune	Graminoid Dune
	Herbaceous Dune
Sparse Vegetation	Sparse Vegetation-Sand
	Beach
	Coral Rubble
Non-Vegetative	Human Impacted
	Open Water

Table 6. Vegetation classification

I. Woodland (S. Fla)

    A. Mangrove Woodland (S. Fla)

        1. Black Mangrove Woodland (S. Fla)

            Avicennia germinans Woodland (DRTO)

        2. Buttonwood Woodland (S. Fla)

            Conocarpus erectus Woodland (DRTO)

    B. Upland Woodland (S. Fla)

        1. Coastal Hardwood Woodland (DRTO)

           i. Seagrape Woodland (DRTO)

            Coccoloba uvifera Woodland (DRTO)

II. Shrubland (S. Fla)

    A. Mangrove Shrubland (S. Fla)

        1. Black Mangrove Shrubland (S. Fla)

            Avicennia germinans Shrubland (DRTO)

        2. Buttonwood Shrubland (S. Fla)

            Conocarpus erectus Shrubland (DRTO)

        3. Mixed Mangrove Shrubland (S. Fla)

           i. Black Mangrove-White Mangrove Shrubland (S. Fla)

            Avicennia germinans-Laguncularia racemosa Mangrove Shrubland (DRTO)

    B. Upland Shrubland (S. Fla)

        1. Coastal Shrubland (S. Fla)

           i. Orange Geigertree Shrubland (DRTO)

            Cordia sebestena Shrubland (DRTO)

           ii. Bay Cedar Shrubland (DRTO)

            Suriana maritima Shrubland (DRTO)

           iii. Sea Lavender Shrubland (DRTO)

            Argusia gnaphalodes Shrubland (DRTO)

           iv. Seagrape Shrubland (DRTO)

            Coccoloba uvifera Shrubland (DRTO)

        2. Mixed Coastal Shrubland (DRTO)

           i. Sea Lavender-Bay Cedar Shrubland Alliance (DRTO)

            Argusia gnaphalodes-Suriana maritima Shrubland Alliance (DRTO)

III. Scrub (S. Fla)

    A. Mangrove Scrub (S. Fla)

        1. White Mangrove Scrub (S. Fla)

            Laguncularia racemosa Scrub (DRTO)

        2. Red Mangrove Scrub (S. Fla)

            Rhizophora mangle Scrub (DRTO)

        3. Buttonwood Scrub (S. Fla)

            Conocarpus erectus Scrub (DRTO)

    B. Upland Scrub (S. Fla)

        1. Upland Scrub (S. Fla)

           i. Bay Cedar Scrub

            Suriana maritima Scrub (DRTO)

           ii. Sea Lavender Scrub (DRTO)

            Argusia gnaphalodes Scrub (DRTO)

IV. Dune (S. Fla)

    A. Graminoid Dune (S. Fla)

       1. Sandbur (S. Fla)

            Cenchrus myosuroides Dune Association (DRTO)

       2. Seaoats (S. Fla)

            Uniola paniculata Dune Association (DRTO)

       3. Pinewoods Fingergrass (DRTO)

            Eustachys petraea Dune Association (DRTO)

       4. Seashore Dropseed (DRTO)

            Sporobolus virginicus Dune Association (DRTO)

       5. Coral Dropseed (DRTO)

            Sporobolus domingensis Dune Association (DRTO)

       6. Flatleaf Flatsedge (DRTO)

            Cyperus planifolius Dune Association (DRTO)

    B. Herbaceous Dune (S. Fla)

       1. Railroad Vine (S. Fla)

            Ipomoea pes-caprae Dune Association (DRTO)

       2. Moonflower (DRTO)

            Ipomoea alba Dune Association (DRTO)

       3. Erect Pricklypear Cactus (DRTO)

            Opuntia stricta Dune Association (DRTO)

       4. Mangrove Spiderlily (DRTO)

            Hymenocallis latifolia Dune Association (DRTO)

       5. Beach Sandmat (DRTO)

            Chamaesyce mesembrianthemifolia Dune Association (DRTO)

       6. Sea Purslane (DRTO)

            Sesuvium portulacastrum Dune Association (DRTO)

       7. Snow Squarestem (DRTO)

            Melanthera nivea Dune Association (DRTO)

       8. Little Hogweed (DRTO)

            Portulaca oleracea Dune Association (DRTO)

       9. Coastal Searocket (DRTO)

            Cakile lanceolata Dune Association (DRTO)

      10. Crested Saltbush (DRTO)

            Atriplex pentandra Dune Association (DRTO)

      11. Mixed Herbaceous Dune (DRTO)

        i. Erect Pricklypear Cactus-Mangrove Spiderlily (DRTO)

            Opuntia stricta-Hymenocallis latifolia Dune Alliance (DRTO)

        ii. Erect Pricklypear Cactus-Moonflower (DRTO)

            Opuntia stricta-Ipomoea alba Dune Alliance (DRTO)

        iii. Seacoast Marshelder-Beach Sandmat-Seaoats (DRTO)

            Iva imbricata-Chamaesyce mesembrianthemifolia-Uniola paniculata Dune Alliance (DRTO)

        iv. Mixed Dune Species (DRTO)

V. Sparse Vegetation (DRTO)

    A. Sparse Vegetation-Sand (DRTO)

    B. Beach (DRTO)

    C. Coral Rubble (DRTO)

VI. Non-Vegetative (S. Fla)

    A. Human Impacted (S. Fla)

       1. Human Impacted Area (DRTO)

    B. Open Water (S. Fla)

       1. Salt Pond (DRTO)

Table 7. Vegetation mapping class statistics

Vegetation Class	Number of Polygons	Total Area (m²)	Average Area (m²)	Minimum Area (m²)	Maximum Area (m²)
Bush Key	**206**	**64383**	**313**	**1**	**8222**
Argusia gnaphalodes Scrub	3	27	9	4	17
Argusia gnaphalodes Shrubland	43	2807	65	4	427
Argusia gnaphalodes-Suriana maritima Shrubland Alliance	6	860	143	12	584
Atriplex pentandra Dune Association	6	412	69	2	176
Avicennia germinans-Laguncularia racemosa Mangrove Shrubland	1	51	51	51	51
Beach	25	8724	349	2	7700
Cakile lanceolata Dune Association	9	7852	872	5	4159
Chamaesyce mesembrianthemifolia Dune Association	18	5230	291	1	1693
Coccoloba uvifera Shrubland	1	25	25	25	25
Conocarpus erectus Scrub	1	34	34	34	34
Coral Rubble	10	8334	833	1	8222
Ipomoea pes-caprae Dune Association	1	176	176	176	176
Melanthera nivea Dune Association	5	4180	836	2	3832
Mixed Dune Species	25	7366	295	5	1516
Opuntia stricta Dune Association	11	2326	211	3	941
Portulaca oleracea Dune Association	2	3808	1904	249	3559
Salt Pond	1	405	405	405	405
Sesuvium portulacastrum Dune Association	21	3281	156	21	533
Sparse Vegetation-Sand	7	7401	1057	86	3847
Sporobolus domingensis Dune Association	2	144	72	66	77
Sporobolus virginicus Dune Association	1	77	77	77	77
Suriana maritima Scrub	2	54	27	11	43
Suriana maritima Shrubland	4	510	127	13	432
Uniola paniculata Dune Association	1	298	298	298	298
East Key	**14**	**23287**	**1663**	**16**	**9085**
Beach	5	18284	3657	16	9085
Ipomoea pes-caprae Dune Association	1	104	104	104	104
Sparse Vegetation-Sand	8	4899	612	16	3253
Garden Key	**22**	**90037**	**4093**	**36**	**63708**
Beach	3	6429	2143	1551	2963
Coccoloba uvifera Shrubland	2	123	61	36	86
Coccoloba uvifera Woodland	5	727	145	103	185
Conocarpus erectus Woodland	5	2250	450	153	1149
Human Impacted Area	4	68879	17220	60	63708
Ipomoea pes-caprae Dune Association	1	281	281	281	281

Vegetation Class	Number of Polygons	Total Area (m²)	Average Area (m²)	Minimum Area (m²)	Maximum Area (m²)
Opuntia stricta-Hymenocallis latifolia Dune Alliance	1	81	81	81	81
Sporobolus virginicus Dune Association	1	11268	11268	11268	11268
Hospital Key	**3**	**3667**	**1222**	**1003**	**1460**
Beach	3	3667	1222	1003	1460
Loggerhead Key	**145**	**197547**	**1362**	**7**	**52424**
Argusia gnaphalodes Scrub	7	434	62	36	105
Argusia gnaphalodes Shrubland	25	22326	893	48	4177
Argusia gnaphalodes-Suriana maritima Shrubland Alliance	3	740	247	26	399
Beach	8	53719	6715	7	52424
Cenchrus myosuroides Dune Association	1	83	83	83	83
Chamaesyce mesembrianthemifolia Dune Association	4	1022	255	82	493
Coccoloba uvifera Shrubland	2	555	278	113	443
Conocarpus erectus Shrubland	1	66	66	66	66
Cordia sebestena Shrubland	2	2321	1161	707	1614
Cyperus planifolius Dune Association	1	183	183	183	183
Eustachys petraea Dune Association	3	1861	620	79	1506
Human Impacted Area	4	14630	3658	545	11127
Hymenocallis latifolia Dune Association	2	104	52	25	79
Ipomoea alba Dune Association	5	3937	787	102	2659
Iva imbricata-Chamaesyce mesembrianthemifolia-Uniola paniculata Dune Alliance	4	17978	4495	47	17397
Melanthera nivea Dune Association	1	334	334	334	334
Opuntia stricta Dune Association	8	13582	1698	18	7763
Opuntia stricta-Hymenocallis latifolia Dune Alliance	9	7324	814	33	4595
Opuntia stricta-Ipomoea alba Dune Alliance	4	23854	5964	1095	16063
Sesuvium portulacastrum Dune Association	6	1475	246	111	485
Sparse Vegetation-Sand	14	14324	1023	43	3385
Sporobolus virginicus Dune Association	2	1425	713	432	993
Suriana maritima Shrubland	24	12645	527	22	6331
Uniola paniculata Dune Association	5	2622	524	40	1669
Long Key	**45**	**10921**	**243**	**0.5**	**3613**
Argusia gnaphalodes Scrub	1	12	12	12	12
Argusia gnaphalodes Shrubland	4	69	17	8	33
Avicennia germinans Shrubland	3	92	31	17	39
Avicennia germinans Woodland	11	1278	116	1	721
Chamaesyce mesembrianthemifolia Dune Association	5	1801	360	20	1567

44

Vegetation Class	Number of Polygons	Total Area (m²)	Average Area (m²)	Minimum Area (m²)	Maximum Area (m²)
Coral Rubble	13	7326	564	0.5	3613
Ipomoea alba Dune Association	1	87	87	87	87
Laguncularia racemosa Scrub	1	24	24	24	24
Portulaca oleracea Dune Association	3	65	22	15	26
Rhizophora mangle Scrub	1	11	11	11	11
Sesuvium portulacastrum Dune Association	1	139	139	139	139
Suriana maritima Scrub	1	17	17	17	17
Middle Key	**3**	**3854**	**1285**	**756**	**1675**
Beach	3	3854	1285	756	1675
Grand Total	**438**	**393696**	**899**	**0.5**	**63708**

Table 8. Community presence across islands (as given by the number of map polygons)

Row Labels	Bush Key	East Key	Garden Key	Hospital Key	Loggerhead Key	Long Key	Middle Key	Grand Total
Argusia gnaphalodes Scrub	3				7	1		11
Argusia gnaphalodes Shrubland	43				25	4		72
Argusia gnaphalodes-Suriana maritima Shrubland Alliance	6				3			9
Atriplex pentandra Dune Association	6							6
Avicennia germinans Shrubland						3		3
Avicennia germinans Woodland						11		11
Avicennia germinans-Laguncularia racemosa Mangrove Shrubland	1							1
Beach	25	5	3	3	8		3	47
Cakile lanceolata Dune Association	9							9
Cenchrus myosuroides Dune Association					1			1
Chamaesyce mesembrianthemifolia Dune Association	18				4	5		27
Coccoloba uvifera Shrubland	1		2		2			5
Coccoloba uvifera Woodland			5					5
Conocarpus erectus Scrub	1							1
Conocarpus erectus Shrubland					1			1
Conocarpus erectus Woodland			5					5
Coral Rubble	10					13		23
Cordia sebestena Shrubland					2			2
Cyperus planifolius Dune Association					1			1
Eustachys petraea Dune Association					3			3
Human Impacted Area			4		4			8
Hymenocallis latifolia Dune Association					2			2
Ipomoea alba Dune Association					5	1		6
Ipomoea pes-caprae Dune Association	1	1	1					3
Iva imbricata-Chamaesyce mesembrianthemifolia-Uniola paniculata Dune Alliance					4			4
Laguncularia racemosa Scrub						1		1
Melanthera nivea Dune Association	5				1			6
Mixed Dune Species	25							25
Opuntia stricta Dune Association	11				8			19
Opuntia stricta-Hymenocallis latifolia Dune Alliance			1		9			10
Opuntia stricta-Ipomoea alba Dune Alliance					4			4
Portulaca oleracea Dune Association	2					3		5
Rhizophora mangle Scrub						1		1
Salt Pond	1							1
Sesuvium portulacastrum Dune Association	21				6	1		28
Sparse Vegetation-Sand	7	8			14			29

Row Labels	Bush Key	East Key	Garden Key	Hospital Key	Loggerhead Key	Long Key	Middle Key	Grand Total
Sporobolus domingensis Dune Association	2							2
Sporobolus virginicus Dune Association	1		1		2			4
Suriana maritima Scrub	2					1		3
Suriana maritima Shrubland	4				24			28
Uniola paniculata Dune Association	1				5			6
Grand Total	**206**	**14**	**22**	**3**	**145**	**45**	**3**	**438**

Table 9. Field descriptions of the vegetation polygons feature class

Field Name	Description
OBJECTID	Automatic numbering of polygons by ArcMap GIS
Shape	Geometric information of the polygon
Island	Island which the polygon is in
Species	Species found within the polygon
Unit_Mark	GPS unit number combined with GPS mark number
L1_Class	The highest and most basic level of the hierarchy; found in Rutchey *et al.* (2006)
L2_Type	Modifies the structurally-defined Level 1 with a community designation; found in Rutchey *et al.* (2006) and Ruiz *et al.* (2008) with additions by SFCN
L3_Group	Identified by dominant species prior to the community designation from Level 2; found in Rutchey *et al.* (2006) and Ruiz *et al.* (2008) with additions by SFCN
L4_Formation	Subdivision of the previous community types by dominant canopy species composition and then by understory species assemblages; found in Rutchey *et al.* (2006) and Ruiz *et al.* (2008) with additions by SFCN
L5_Alliance	Subdivision of the previous community types by dominant canopy species composition and then by understory species assemblages; found in Rutchey *et al.* (2006) and Ruiz *et al.* (2008) with additions by SFCN
L6_Association	Subdivision of the previous community types by dominant canopy species composition and then by understory species assemblages; found in Rutchey *et al.* (2006) and Ruiz *et al.* (2008) with additions by SFCN
GPS_Date	Date that the GPS mark was taken
Veg_Type	Vegetation code number used during field mapping
Trimble_Comment	Comments entered in the Trimble GeoXT about polygon shape, composition, and general mapping remarks
Data_Comment	Comments written about the polygon
Delineator	Person who mapped the polygon
Pictures	Number of photos pertaining to polygon
X_Coordinate	UTM easting (x) centroid coordinate based on Zone 17 North
Y_Coordinate	UTM northing (y) centroid coordinate based on Zone 17 North
Shape_Length	Perimeter length of the polygon in meters
Shape_Area	Area of the polygon in square meters
PolyID	The polygon's unique identifier

Table 10. Field descriptions of the field plots feature class

Field Name	Description
OBJECTID	Number of point automatically assigned by ArcMap GIS
Shape	Geometric information of the point
Unit_Mark	GPS unit number combined with GPS mark number
Island	Island which the field plot is located in
GPS_Date	Date the GPS mark was taken
Veg_Type	Vegetation code number used during field mapping
Species	Species found in field plot
Trimble_Comment	Comments entered in the Trimble GeoXT about polygon shape, composition, and general mapping remarks
Data_Comment	Comments written about the polygon which the field plot is located in
Delineator	Person who mapped the polygon which the field plot is located in
Pictures	Number of photos pertaining to field plots
X_Coordinate	UTM easting (x) centroid coordinate based on Zone 17 North
Y_Coordinate	UTM northing (y) centroid coordinate based on Zone 17 North

Table 11. Vegetation types used for field mapping

Vegetation Type	Description	Common Names
1	Human Impacted Area	-
2	*Opuntia stricta*	erect pricklypear cactus
3	*Opuntia stricta-Hymenocallis latifolia*	erect pricklypear cactus-mangrove spiderlily
4	*Opuntia stricta-Ipomoea alba*	erect pricklypear cactus-moonflower
5	*Cordia sebestena*	orange geiger tree
6	*Uniola paniculata*	seaoats
7	*Cenchrus myosuroides*	giant sandbur
8	*Suriana maritima*	bay cedar
9	*Conocarpus erectus*	buttonwood
10	*Argusia gnaphalodes-Suriana maritima*	sea lavender-bay cedar
11	*Eustachys petraea*	pinewoods fingergrass
12	*Coccoloba uvifera*	sea grape
13	*Iva imbricata-Chamaesyce mesembrianthemifolia-Uniola paniculata*	seacoast marshelder-beach sandmat-seaoats
14	*Sporobolus virginicus*	seashore dropseed
15	*Argusia gnaphalodes*	sea lavender
16	Sparse Vegetation-Sand	-
17	*Sesuvium portulacastrum*	sea purslane
18	*Ipomoea alba* and/or *Ipomoea pes-caprae*	moonflower and/or railroad vine
19	*Cyperus planifolius*	flatleaf flatsedge
20	*Chamaesyce mesembrianthemifolia*	beach sandmat
21	*Hymenocallis latifolia*	mangrove spiderlily
22	Beach	-
23	*Melanthera nivea*	snow squarestem
24	*Portulaca oleracea*	little hogweed
25	Coral Rubble	-
26	*Avicennia-Laguncularia*	black-white mangrove
27	*Avicennia germinans*	black mangrove
28	Mixed Dune Species	-
29	*Laguncularia racemosa*	white mangrove
30	*Rhizophora mangle*	red mangrove
31	*Cakile lanceolata*	coastal searocket
32	*Atriplex pentandra*	crested saltbush
33	*Sporobolus domingensis*	coral dropseed
34	Salt Pond	-

Table 12. Species relative abundance across five transects compared to the mapped vegetation classes

	Transect species	Vegetation Map Communities	Transect %	Veg Map %
Comparable	Opuntia stricta	Opuntia stricta Dune Association		11.82
		Opuntia stricta-Hymenocallis latifolia Dune Alliance	20.71	6.38
		Opuntia stricta-Ipomoea alba Dune Alliance		20.77
	Ipomoea alba	Ipomoea alba Dune Association	22.95	3.43
	Hymenocallis latifolia	Hymenocallis latifolia Dune Association	0.58	0.09
	TOTAL	**TOTAL**	**44.24**	**42.49**
	Argusia gnaphalodes	Argusia gnaphalodes Scrub		0.38
		Argusia gnaphalodes Shrubland	14.59	19.44
		Argusia gnaphalodes-Suriana maritima Shrubland Alliance		0.64
	Suriana maritima	Suriana maritima Shrubland	10.01	11.01
	TOTAL	**TOTAL**	**24.60**	**31.47**
	Iva imbricata	Iva imbricata-C. mesembrianthemifolia-Uniola paniculata Dune Alliance	5.90	15.65
	C. mesembrianthemifolia	Chamaesyce mesembrianthemifolia Dune Association	1.53	0.89
	Uniola paniculata	Uniola paniculata Dune Association	6.47	2.28
	TOTAL	**TOTAL**	**13.90**	**18.82**
	Sesuvium portulacastrum	Sesuvium portulacastrum Dune Association	3.15	1.28
	Eustachys petraea	Eustachys petraea Dune Association	2.46	1.62
	Cordia sebestena	Cordia sebestena Shrubland	2.02	2.02
	Melanthera nivea	Melanthera nivea Dune Association	1.84	0.29
	Cyperus planifolius	Cyperus planifolius Dune Association	0.67	0.16
Transect Only	Canavalia rosea		3.79	0
	Ambrosia hispida		2.40	0
	Cakile lanceolata		0.42	0
	Ipomoea pes-caprae		0.20	0
	Capraria biflora		0.13	0
	Lepidium virginicum		0.13	0
	Scaevola plumieri		0.04	0
	Conyza canadensis		0.02	0
Map Only		Sporobolus virginicus Dune Association	0	1.24
		Coccoloba uvifera Shrubland	0	0.48
		Cenchrus myosuroides Dune Association	0	0.07
		Conocarpus erectus Shrubland	0	0.06

Table 13. Species relative abundance across compared to the mapped vegetation classes, broken down per transect

Transect	Species	Vegetation Map Communities	Transect %	Veg Map %
1	*Ipomoea alba*	*Ipomoea alba* Dune Association	18.67	28.70
	Opuntia stricta	*Opuntia stricta-Ipomoea alba* Dune Alliance	8.34	13.94
		Opuntia stricta Dune Association		17.25
	TOTAL		**27.01**	**59.89**
	Argusia gnaphalodes	*Argusia gnaphalodes* Shrubland	15.73	26.88
	Eustachys petraea	*Eustachys petraea* Dune Association	10.72	7.08
	Sesuvium portulacastrum	*Sesuvium portulacastrum* Dune Association	9.69	1.66
	Melanthera nivea	*Melanthera nivea* Dune Association	1.59	4.50
	Canavalia rosea		16.52	
	Iva imbricata		7.55	
	Ambrosia hispida		4.37	
	Uniola paniculata		2.30	
	Cyperus planifolius		1.99	
	Cakile lanceolata		1.83	
	Suriana maritima		0.64	
	C. mesembrianthemifolia		0.08	
4	*Opuntia stricta*	*Opuntia stricta* Dune Association	24.34	44.70
	Argusia gnaphalodes	*Argusia gnaphalodes* Shrubland	15.76	27.66
	Suriana maritima	*Suriana maritima* Shrubland	13.11	23.48
	Iva imbricata	*Iva imbricata-C. mesembrianthemifolia-Uniola paniculata* Dune Alliance	5.74	4.16
	C. mesembrianthemifolia		0.38	
	Uniola paniculata		0.38	
	TOTAL		**6.49**	**4.16**
	Ipomoea alba		35.31	
	Ambrosia hispida		4.85	
	Scaevola plumieri		0.13	
7	*Iva imbricata*	*Iva imbricata-C. mesembrianthemifolia-Uniola paniculata* Dune Alliance	17.14	53.13
	C. mesembrianthemifolia		0.25	
	Uniola paniculata		39.75	
	TOTAL		**57.14**	**53.13**
	Suriana maritima	*Suriana maritima* Shrubland	37.88	25.92
	Opuntia stricta	*Opuntia stricta-Ipomoea alba* Dune Alliance	3.12	20.95
	Ipomoea alba		1.49	
	TOTAL		**4.61**	**20.95**
	Cyperus planifolius		0.37	
11	*Opuntia stricta*	*Opuntia stricta-Ipomoea alba* Dune Alliance	31.34	62.46
	Ipomoea alba	*Opuntia stricta-Hymenocallis latifolia* Dune Alliance	25.20	4.36
	Hymenocallis latifolia		0.92	
	TOTAL		**57.47**	**66.83**

51

Transect	Species	Vegetation Map Communities	Transect %	Veg Map %
	Argusia gnaphalodes	Argusia gnaphalodes Shrubland	13.59	11.99
	Cordia sebestena	Cordia sebestena Shrubland	10.26	10.84
	Sesuvium portulacastrum	Sesuvium portulacastrum Dune Association	4.72	2.28
	Melanthera nivea		7.49	
	C. mesembrianthemifolia		3.24	
	Ipomoea pes-caprae		1.02	
	Cyperus planifolius		0.83	
	Capraria biflora		0.65	
	Lepidium virginicum		0.65	
	Conyza canadensis		0.09	
		Suriana maritima Shrubland		8.07
	Opuntia stricta	Opuntia stricta-Ipomoea alba Dune Alliance	37.10	67.74
	Ipomoea alba	Opuntia stricta-Hymenocallis latifolia Dune Alliance	23.81	4.75
	Hymenocallis latifolia		2.89	
	TOTAL	TOTAL	63.81	72.50
12	Argusia gnaphalodes	Argusia gnaphalodes Shrubland	27.10	24.78
		Argusia gnaphalodes Scrub		2.72
	TOTAL	TOTAL	27.10	27.50
	C. mesembrianthemifolia		5.28	
	Suriana maritima		3.82	

Table 14. Dry Tortugas National Park vegetation mapping project products or file descriptions and filenames. Naming conventions and required files follow guidelines from the NPS Vegetation Mapping Inventory Program.

Category	Product or File Description	Filename
Aerial Photography	*(Not applicable)*	
Project Report	Project report (contains full report about the vegetation map including funding source, background information, methods and results, final product specifications, brief description of products and files, vegetation classification and key, map class descriptions, photos of map classes, and example field data sheets)	drtorpt.pdf drtorpt_pressquality.pdf
Field Data	Graphics showing location of field sites MS Excel format of polygon field data Field polygon photos (photos named using Island and PolyID fields found in plots.xls, i.e., *Island_PolyID ....*)	drtoplots.pdf plots.xls field_photos.zip

Geospatial Vegetation Information	Zip folder containing geodatabase (drto.mdb) of spatial data (includes data for vegetation polygons, field points and polygon data, park boundary, and shoreline)
	ESRI ArcMap Project file – displays geodatabase (MDB) files
	Graphics of vegetation communities (low resolution)
	Graphics of vegetation communities (high resolution)
	Although use of the geodatabase and ArcMap Project File is recommended, individual shapefiles are also included as zip files:
	    Vegetation polygons
	    Field plots
	    Park boundary
	    Shoreline
		drto.zip
		
		drto_veg_project.mxd
		
		drto.pdf
		drto_large.pdf
		
		drto_vegetation_polygons.zip
		drto_field_plots.zip
		drto_boundary.zip
		drto_shoreline.zip

Accuracy Assessment Information	*(Not applicable)*	
Project Metadata	Spatial vegetation metadata Field plots metadata Park boundary metadata Shoreline metadata	metadrtospatial.txt metadrtofield.txt metadrtobdy.txt metadrtoshl.txt

Literature Cited

Agassiz, Alexander. 1883. Explorations of the surface fauna of the Gulf Stream, under the auspices of the United States Coast Survey. II. The Tortugas and Florida reefs. Mem. Amer. Acad. Arts Sci. Centennial, Vol. II: 107-132.

Bowman, H.H.M. 1918. Botanical ecology of the Dry Tortugas. *Papers Tortugas Laboratory* 12: 109-38

Davis, J.H., Jr. 1940. The ecology and geologic role of mangroves in Florida. *Papers Tortugas Lab*. 32: 303-412.

Davis, J.H. Jr. 1942. The ecology of the vegetation and topography of the Sand Keys of Florida. *Papers Tortugas Laboratory* 33: 113-95.

Davis, R.A. Jr. and C.W. O'Neill. 1979. Morphodynamics of East Key, Dry Tortugas, Florida. *in Guide to Sedimentation for the Dry Tortugas, Fort Jefferson National Monument Florida Southeast Geological Society Publication* 21: 7-13.

Doyle, T.W., T.C. Michot, R.H. Day, and C.J. Wells. 2002. History and ecology of mangroves in the Dry Tortugas: Lafayette, LA, National Wetlands Research Center, United States Geological Survey, Fact Sheet 047-02.

Everglades National Park. 1993. Loggerhead Key vegetation map. Unpublished document.

Gauld, G. 1790. *An accurate chart of the Tortugas and Florida Keys or Martyrs, surveyed by George Gauld, A.M. in the years 1773, 1774, and 1775*. London: W. Faden. 2nd edition, 1820.

Millspaugh, C.F. 1907. Flora of the sand keys of Florida. *Columbian Museum* 118, no. (Bot. Ser. 2): 191-245.

National Park Service. 1994 Draft. Dry Tortugas National Park resource management plan, 1994.

National Park Service 1999. Dry Tortugas National Park, 1999 annual report. Available online at http://www.nps.gov/drto/parkmgmt/upload/drto1999annualreport.pdf. National Park Service, Homestead, FL. 18 pp.

National Park Service 2000. Dry Tortugas National Park, 2000 annual report. Available online at http://www.nps.gov/drto/parkmgmt/upload/drto2000annualreport.pdf. National Park Service, Homestead, FL. 16 pp.

Pendleton, E.A., E.R. Thieler, and S.J. Williams. 2005. Coastal vulnerability assessment of Dry Tortugas National Park to sea-level rise. United States Geological Survey, Open-File Report 2004-1416. Available online at http://pubs.usgs.gov/of/2004/1416/index.html.

Pernas, T., B. Gamble and T.V. Armentano. 2001. Dry Tortugas National Park, Loggerhead Key exotic plant management and island restoration project. *Wildland Weeds*. Winter 2001: 13-17

Reimus, R.G. and W.B. Robertson. 2001. Plants of Bush Key, Dry Tortugas National Park. Unpublished plant list.

Robertson, W.B. Jr. 1964. The terns of the Dry Tortugas. *Bulletin of the State Museum, Biological Museum* 8, no. 1: 1-95.

Roth, C., Jr. Date unknown. Role of Key West and the Dry Tortugas in the military history of the United States during the nineteenth century. Rare Book Collection, Everglades National Park, Florida.

Ruiz, P.L., P.A. Houle, M.S. Ross. 2008. The 2008 terrestrial vegetation of Biscayne National Park, Fl, USA derived from aerial photography, NDVI, and LiDAR. Southeast Environmental Research Center, Miami, Fl 33199. 62 pp.

Rutchey, K., T.N. Schall, R.F. Doren, A. Atkinson, M.S. Ross, D.T. Jones, M. Madden, L. Vilchek, K.A. Bradley, J.R. Snyder, J.N. Burch, T. Pernas, B. Witcher, M. Pyne, R. White, T.J. Smith III, J. Sadle, C.S. Smith, M.E. Patterson, and G.D. Gann. 2006. Vegetation classification for South Florida natural areas: Saint Petersburg, Fl, United States Geological Survey, Open-File Report 2006-1240. 142 pp.

Sadle, J. 2007 Draft. Vegetation management in Dry Tortugas National Park, September 2007. South Florida Natural Resources Center, Everglades National Park, 40001 SR 9336, Homestead, Fl 33034. 5 pp.

Schmidt, T.W. and L. Pikula. 1997. Scientific studies on Dry Tortugas National Park: an annotated bibliography. *Atoll Research Bulletin* 449: 1-124.

Schroeder, P.B. and J.H. Davis. 1971. Ecology vegetation and topography of the Dry Tortugas updated to 1970. *Quarterly Journal of the Florida Academy of Science* (Suppl 1): 12-13.

Sprunt, A. Jr. 1948. The tern colonies of the Dry Tortugas keys. *Auk* 65: 1-19.

Stoddart, D.R. and F.R. Fosberg. 1981. Topographic and floristic change, Dry Tortugas, Florida, 1904-1977. *Atoll Research Bulletin* 253: 1-56.

Thornberry-Ehrlich, T.L. 2005. Dry Tortugas National Park geologic resource management issues scoping summary. Colorado State University – Geologic Resource Evaluation. February 9, 2005.

Appendix A. Vegetation Classifications

Human Impacted Area

Name, translated: Human Impacted Area
Vegetation (Dry Tortugas National Park):
> A disturbed site with an undefined community type consisting of *Melanthera nivea, Chamaesyce mesembrianthemifolia, Cocos nucifera, Conyza canadensis var. pusilla, Stachytarpheta jamaicensis, Argusia gnaphalodes, Suriana maritima, Phoenix dactylifera* and *Iva imbricata.*

Environment (Dry Tortugas National Park):
> An area of disturbed land found around the surrounding area of the lighthouse and park housing on Loggerhead Key. Human impacted areas are also found in and around Fort Jefferson on Garden Key. These areas are subjected to high visitor and/or staff foot traffic and may also be subjected to administrative activities including grounds maintenance and other operations involving motorized vehicles.

Opuntia stricta Dune Association

Name, translated: Erect Pricklypear Cactus Dune Association
Vegetation (Dry Tortugas National Park):

> Coastal herbaceous community dominated by the succulent *Opuntia stricta* (erect pricklypear). This community can occur in near monotypic stands and lacks a tree or shrub overstory. Other species found in this habitat include low densities of *Ipomoea alba* and *Cyperus planifolius.* On Bush Key, this community is more mixed including other species such as *Melanthera nivea, Chamaesyce mesembrianthemifolia,* and *Argusia gnaphalodes.* Canopy height ranges from 0.5 to 1 m. Canopy cover ranges from 20% to 100%.

Environment (Dry Tortugas National Park):

> Found on sandy substrates in the interior of Loggerhead Key. This vegetation type is also found in the interior of Bush Key on the west and east sides of the island.

Opuntia stricta-Hymenocallis latifolia **Dune Alliance**

Name, translated: Erect Pricklypear Cactus-Mangrove Spiderlily Dune Alliance
Vegetation (Dry Tortugas National Park):

Coastal community dominated by herbaceous to semi-woody succulent *Opuntia stricta* and the succulent *Hymenocallis latifolia*. No overstory species present. Other species commonly found in this habitat include *Chamaesyce mesembrianthemifolia, Sporobolus indicus, Aloe vera, Agave sisalana* and low densities of *Ipomoea alba.* Canopy height ranges from 1 to 1.5 m. Canopy cover ranges from 20% to 100%.

Environment (Dry Tortugas National Park):

This community is generally found on Loggerhead Key in patches on beach dunes and in areas south and north of the lighthouse. This community is also found on Garden Key.

Opuntia stricta-Ipomoea alba Dune Alliance

Name, translated: Erect Pricklypear Cactus-Moonflower Dune Alliance
Vegetation (Dry Tortugas National Park):

> Low growing mix of the herbaceous to semi-woody succulent *Opuntia stricta* and high densities of the herbaceous vine *Ipomoea alba*. No overstory species present. This community may also include *Cyperus planifolius*. The moonflower vine *Ipomoea alba*, in many instances, will be climbing over the *Opuntia stricta*. Canopy height ranges from 0.5 to 1 m. Canopy cover ranges from 20% to 100%.

Environment (Dry Tortugas National Park):

> This community is generally found in large patches in the interior portion of Loggerhead Key.

Cordia sebestena **Shrubland**

Name, translated: Orange Geigertree Shrubland
Vegetation (Dry Tortugas National Park):
    A coastal shrub dominated community of *Cordia sebestena* with a canopy height ranging from 2 to 3 m. Understory species include *Opuntia stricta* and *Cakile lanceolata* and is generally 1 to 2 m in height.
Environment (Dry Tortugas National Park):
    This community exists in two patches on opposite sides of Loggerhead Key on the edges of dunes. Many taller snags may be associated with this community representing dieback of the trees due to hurricanes.

Uniola paniculata **Dune Association**

Name, translated: Seaoats Dune Association
Vegetation (Dry Tortugas National Park):
 Coastal dune community dominated by the large herbaceous grass Uniola paniculata. This community has a canopy height ranging from 1-1.5 m up to 2 m or more when in flower. Other species present in this community include *Opuntia stricta, Chamaesyce mesembrianthemifolia, Suriana maritima,* and low densities of *Ipomoea alba.*
Environment (Dry Tortugas National Park):
 This community is found along edges of beach dunes on Loggerhead Key and the interior of western Bush Key.

Cenchrus myosuroides Dune Association

Name, translated: Giant Sandbur Dune Association
Vegetation (Dry Tortugas National Park):
    Beach dune community consisting mostly of the large perennial grass *Cenchrus myosuroides*. This large graminoid is a rare species found in a couple counties in southwest Florida. This community had an understory of *Opuntia stricta*. The canopy height was about 1-1.5 m tall with an understory canopy up to 1 m.
Environment (Dry Tortugas National Park):
    This community was found once on a beach dune near the lighthouse on the east side of Loggerhead Key.

***Suriana maritima* Shrubland/Scrub**

Name, translated: Bay Cedar Shrubland/Scrub
Vegetation (Dry Tortugas National Park):

A coastal shrubland dominated by *Suriana maritima.* Other shrub species include *Argusia gnaphalodes, Iva imbricata,* and *Caesalpinia bonduc.* Understory species may include *Hymenocallis latifolia, Chamaesyce mesembrianthemifolia, Opuntia stricta* and *Ipomoea alba.* The shrub canopy height ranges from 2 to 3 m with understory heights reaching approximately 1 m. The canopy height is shorter on Bush and Long Key. The scrub community consists of stunted bushes of *Suriana* with varied cover of about 30% to 50%. Associative species may consist of *Chamaesyce mesembrianthemifolia* and *Argusia gnaphalodes.*

Environment (Dry Tortugas National Park):

The shrubland community is widely distributed throughout Loggerhead Key. This community is common on beach dunes, usually behind an *Argusia gnaphalodes* community, and in the interior of Loggerhead Key. This community is also found on eastern Bush Key. The scrub community is found in two locations on Bush Key, near the isthmus and near the boundary between Bush and Long Key, and on the northern strip of Long Key.

Conocarpus erectus **Woodland/Shrubland/Scrub**

Name, translated: Buttonwood Woodland/Shrubland/Scrub
Vegetation (Dry Tortugas National Park):
  Usually found as buttonwood woodland with a canopy height up to 7 m. The understory
  may consist of *Opuntia stricta, Uniola paniculata, Chamaesyce mesembrianthemifolia,
  Sesuvium portulacastrum,* and *Sporobolus indicus.*
Environment (Dry Tortugas National Park):
  The woodland community is found on Garden Key in the camping area outside of Fort
  Jefferson. The Shrubland community is found on Loggerhead Key as a single shrub about
  3 m tall. A one meter tall scrub community can be found in the interior of eastern Bush
  Key.

***Argusia gnaphalodes-Suriana maritima* Shrubland Alliance**

Name, translated: Sea Lavender-Bay Cedar Shrubland Alliance
Vegetation (Dry Tortugas National Park):
    A coastal shrubland community consisting of a relatively even mix of *Argusia gnaphalodes* and *Suriana maritima*. Other understory species may include *Ipomoea alba, Opuntia stricta, Cordia sebestena, and Chamaesyce mesembrianthemifolia*. The canopy height ranges from 2 to 3 m on Loggerhead Key and shorter on Bush Key.
Environment (Dry Tortugas National Park):
    This is a common community found on the north and east beach dunes of Loggerhead Key. This community is also common on the east side of Bush Key.

Eustachys petraea Dune Association

Name, translated: Pinewoods Fingergrass Dune Association
Vegetation (Dry Tortugas National Park):
>   Patchy communities dominated by the herbaceous grass *Eustachys petraea*. *Opuntia stricta* was present in one of the three patches. The height of this community was about 0.3-0.6 m tall. Canopy cover ranges from 70% to 90%.

Environment (Dry Tortugas National Park):
>   There are three patches that were found in the interior of Loggerhead Key in monotypic stands with the exception of one patch accompanied by low densities of the cactus *Opuntia stricta*.

***Coccoloba uvifera* Woodland/Shrubland**

Name, translated: Seagrape Woodland/Shrubland
Vegetation (Dry Tortugas National Park):
>   Coastal shrubland or woodland dominated by *Coccoloba uvifera.* Canopy height ranges from about 3-4 m tall on Loggerhead Key and 6-7 m tall on Garden Key. Understory species may include *Opuntia stricta, Chamaesyce mesembrianthemifolia, Cakile lanceolata,* and *Melanthera nivea.*

Environment (Dry Tortugas National Park):
>   This community appears as a shrubland in two patches on Loggerhead Key and as a woodland on Garden Key around Fort Jefferson. There is one shrubland community found on the east side of Bush Key.

***Iva imbricata-Chamaesyce mesembrianthemifolia-Uniola paniculata* Dune Alliance**

Name, translated: Seacoast Marshelder-Beach Sandmat-Seaoats Dune Alliance
Vegetation (Dry Tortugas National Park):
> A mixed dune community consisting of *Iva imbricata, Chamaesyce mesembrianthemifolia*, and *Uniola paniculata*. The canopy height ranges from 0.5-1 m with a cover of 30% to 50%.

Environment (Dry Tortugas National Park):
> This community is found on Loggerhead Key in dune habitats that resemble the sparse vegetation community, but differ from it by having higher vegetation cover.

Sporobolus virginicus Dune Alliance

Name, translated: Seashore Dropseed Dune Alliance

Vegetation (Dry Tortugas National Park):

    A community dominated by the small herbaceous grass *Sporobolus virginicus*. Other species associated with this community include *Cakile lanceolata, Chamaesyce mesembrianthemifolia, Opuntia stricta, Hymenocallis latifolia*, and *Argusia gnaphalodes*. Canopy height is low and no taller than 0.3 m. Canopy cover can be up to 80%.

Environment (Dry Tortugas National Park):

    This community is found on Loggerhead Key just south of the lighthouse. On Bush Key, this community is found west of the isthmus. Garden Key has a modified community of *Sporobolus virginicus* Dune Alliance existing in a highly human influenced area.

Argusia gnaphalodes Shrubland/Scrub

Name, translated: Sea Lavender Shrubland/Scrub
Vegetation (Dry Tortugas National Park):

A coastal dune shrub community dominated by *Argusia gnaphalodes*. One of the more diverse communities, the understory may consist of such dune species as *Ipomoea pes-caprae, Sesuvium portulacastrum, Uniola paniculata, Cyperus planifolius, Opuntia stricta, Iva imbricata, Chamaesyce mesembrianthemifolia*, and low densities of *Suriana maritima* and *Ipomoea alba*. Canopy height ranges from 1.5 to 2.5 m. Canopy cover may range from 20% to 100%. On Bush and Long Key, canopy height is shorter and canopy cover is smaller.

Environment (Dry Tortugas National Park):

This is a common community found on beach dunes throughout Loggerhead Key and Bush Key. Loggerhead Key, Bush Key, and Long Key have patchy communities of *Argusia gnaphalodes* existing as a shorter scrub community.

Sparse Vegetation-Sand

Name, translated: Sparse Vegetation-Sand
Vegetation (Dry Tortugas National Park):
      Sparse communities of mixed vegetation with a low percent cover (about 5% to 20%).
      The canopy height is short at about 0.8 m. Species commonly found in this community
      include *Chamaesyce mesembrianthemifolia*, *Cakile lanceolata*, *Iva imbricata*, *Argusia*
      gnaphalodes, and *Suriana maritima*.
Environment (Dry Tortugas National Park):
      Usually found bordering the islands along the shoreline, this sparse community can be
      found on Loggerhead Key, Bush Key, and East Key.

Sesuvium portulacastrum Dune Association

Name, translated: Sea Purslane Dune Association
Vegetation (Dry Tortugas National Park):
> A groundcover beach dune community dominated by the small prostrate herb *Sesuvium portulacastrum*. This mat forming community is generally less than 1 m in height. Other characteristic species include *Opuntia stricta* and *Hymenocallis latifolia*. On Bush Key, other species commonly found in this community include *Chamaesyce mesembrianthemifolia, Atriplex pentandra, Opuntia stricta,* and *Cakile lanceolata.*

Environment (Dry Tortugas National Park):
> This community can be found on beach dunes on Loggerhead Key, eastern and western Bush Key, and a single patch on northern Long Key at the interface with Bush Key.

Ipomoea alba and/or *Ipomoea pes-caprae* Dune Association

Name, translated: Moonflower and/or Railroad Vine Dune Association
Vegetation (Dry Tortugas National Park):

> A coastal dune community dominated by large mats of the herbaceous vines *Ipomoea alba* or *Ipomoea pes-caprae*. In some cases, *Ipomoea alba* will be climbing over and blanketing small patches of *Opuntia stricta*. Other species include *Opuntia stricta*, *Canavalia rosea*, *Cakile lanceolata*, *Distichlis spicata,* and *Chamaesyce mesembrianthemifolia.* This community is no taller than 0.5 m and may have a canopy cover up to 100%.

Environment (Dry Tortugas National Park):

> *Ipomoea pes-caprae* dominated communities are present on Garden Key and East Key. *Ipomoea alba* dominated communities can be found in the interior and western beach dunes of Loggerhead Key. One *Ipomoea alba* community on Loggerhead Key is accompanied by *Ipomoea pes-caprae*. Bush Key has one community of *Ipomoea pes-caprae* on the isthmus. Long Key has an *Ipomoea alba* patch on the southern coast.

Cyperus planifolius **Dune Association**

Name, translated: Flatleaf Flatsedge Dune Association
Vegetation (Dry Tortugas National Park):
    A small dune community dominated by the herbaceous sedge *Cyperus planifolius*. The height of this community is no taller than 1 m. *Ipomoea alba* was present as the understory cover.
Environment (Dry Tortugas National Park):
    There is one community on Loggerhead Key just south of the lighthouse.

Chamaesyce mesembrianthemifolia Dune Association

Name, translated: Beach Sandmat Dune Association

Vegetation (Dry Tortugas National Park):

      Low growing coastal dune community consisting primarily of *Chamaesyce mesembrianthemifolia*. Other species associated with this community include *Distichlis spicata, Melanthera nivea, Ipomoea alba*, and *Cyperus planifolius*. On both Bush and Long Key, this community is more diverse with other species including *Portulaca oleracea, Cyperus planifolius, Sesuvium portulacastrum, Argusia gnaphalodes, Opuntia stricta, and Melanthera nivea.* The canopy height is no taller than 0.5 m. Canopy cover ranges from 20% to 50%.

Environment (Dry Tortugas National Park):

      This community is present on the western beach dunes of Loggerhead Key. This community is more commonly found on Bush and Long Key.

Hymenocallis latifolia Dune Association

Name, translated: Mangrove Spiderlily Dune Association
Vegetation (Dry Tortugas National Park):
> Small coastal dune communities dominated by the succulent *Hymenocallis latifolia*. This community may also include *Sesuvium portulacastrum* and low densities of *Ipomoea alba*. The canopy height is about 1 m tall. Canopy cover ranges from 20% to 80%.

Environment (Dry Tortugas National Park):
> This community is found in the interior of Loggerhead Key.

Beach

Name, translated: Beach
Vegetation (Dry Tortugas National Park):
Areas of mostly open sand with some instances of less than 5% vegetation cover. Very low densities of *Chamaesyce mesembrianthemifolia* and *Cakile lanceolata* may also be found.
Environment (Dry Tortugas National Park):
This can be found on the beaches of Loggerhead Key, Garden Key, Bush Key, Long Key, and East Key. Hospital Key and Middle Key are comprised solely of sand and have no vegetation.

Melanthera nivea Dune Association

Name, translated: Snow Squarestem Dune Association
Vegetation (Dry Tortugas National Park):
    A community consisting primarily of a small to medium herbaceous wildflower
    Melanthera nivea. Found primarily along the coast, this wildflower can grow up to 1 m.
    Other species present in this community includes *Cyperus planifolius* and *Opuntia*
    stricta.
Environment (Dry Tortugas National Park):
    This is an uncommon community found on Loggerhead Key and Bush Key.

***Portulaca oleracea* Dune Association**

Name, translated: Little Hogweed Dune Association
Vegetation (Dry Tortugas National Park):

A small herbaceous wildflower community dominated by *Portulaca oleracea*, this species spreads across the ground and forms small patches. The canopy height is short at about 10 cm tall. Other species present include *Sesuvium portulacastrum*, *Melanthera nivea*, and *Chamaesyce mesembrianthemifolia.*

Environment (Dry Tortugas National Park):

There are two communities on the east and west side of Bush Key. There are three smaller communities on Long Key in the central and southern portion of the island.

Coral Rubble

Name, translated: Coral Rubble

Vegetation (Dry Tortugas National Park):

An area consisting mostly of coral debris with very little or no vegetation, generally less than 5%.

Environment (Dry Tortugas National Park):

Coral debris that has washed ashore on Bush and Long Key. Usually found along the coast of Bush Key, as well as some interior portions of Bush Key. The substrate of Long Key is predominantly made up of coral debris.

***Avicennia germinans-Laguncularia racemosa* Mangrove Shrubland**

Name, translated: Black Mangrove-White Mangrove Shrubland
Vegetation (Dry Tortugas National Park):
Avicennia germinans and *Laguncularia racemosa* dominated community found along the coast in saline environments. This one community was about 2.5 m tall.
Environment (Dry Tortugas National Park):
One community found on the east coast of Bush Key.

Avicennia germinans **Mangrove Woodland/Shrubland**

Name, translated: Black Mangrove Woodland/Shrubland
Vegetation (Dry Tortugas National Park):

A mangrove community dominated by *Avicennia germinans*, and existing as either a woodland or shrubland, based on height. The *Avicennia germinans* woodland is greater than 5 m in height with a canopy cover of 30%. The shrubland community is less than 5 m in height, but canopy cover ranges from 30% to 80%.

Environment (Dry Tortugas National Park):

The woodland community is found on Long Key as the last prominent stand of black mangroves in Dry Tortugas. The shrubland communities are also found on Long Key.

Mixed Dune Species

Name, translated: Mixed Dune Species
Vegetation (Dry Tortugas National Park):
     A community consisting of many interspersed dune species with no one species
     dominating. This diverse community is composed of *Cyperus planifolius, Chamaesyce*
     mesembrianthemifolia, Melanthera nivea, Cakile lanceolata, and *Portulaca oleracea.*
     The canopy height is short (1 m or less) with high canopy cover.
Environment (Dry Tortugas National Park):
     This community is commonly found on western Bush Key.

Laguncularia racemosa **Mangrove Scrub**

Name, translated: White Mangrove Scrub
Vegetation (Dry Tortugas National Park):

A scrub community dominated by *Laguncularia racemosa* with a canopy cover of 90%. This community appears as a recovering habitat where the tree species are less than 1 m tall.

Environment (Dry Tortugas National Park):

Found once on south central Long Key.

Rhizophora mangle Mangrove Scrub

Name, translated: Red Mangrove Scrub
Vegetation (Dry Tortugas National Park):
    This community consists solely of *Rhizophora mangle* within the high tidal zone. The structure of the community is a scrub with a canopy cover of 65%. There are no other species present. The canopy height of the community is 1 m tall.
Environment (Dry Tortugas National Park):
    Rhizophora mangle is found once on Long Key's southern end.

Cakile lanceolata **Dune Association**

Name, translated: Coastal Searocket Dune Association
Vegetation (Dry Tortugas National Park):
  A coastal dune community characterized by the small annual herb *Cakile lanceolata.* The canopy height is less than 1 m tall with cover ranging from 50% to 80%. Other species present are *Portulaca oleracea* and *Chamaesyce mesembrianthemifolia.*
Environment (Dry Tortugas National Park):
  Found in dense stands on western Bush Key.

Atriplex pentandra **Dune Association**

Name, translated: Crested Saltbush Dune Association
Vegetation (Dry Tortugas National Park):
    A dune community dominated by *Atriplex pentandra*. Cover is about 60% to 85%. This
    species-poor community is short in stature (less than 1 m in height).
Environment (Dry Tortugas National Park):
    This community is present in three locations on eastern and western Bush Key.

Sporobolus domingensis Dune Association

Name, translated: Coral Dropseed Dune Association
Vegetation (Dry Tortugas National Park):

A dune community dominated by the grass *Sporobolus domingensis*. This species-poor grass community is short in stature, reaching top heights of less than 1 m.

Environment (Dry Tortugas National Park):

The community exists in two stands in the interior of western Bush Key.

Salt Pond

Name, translated: Salt Pond
Vegetation (Dry Tortugas National Park):
    An ephemeral open water community with little or no vegetation present.
Environment (Dry Tortugas National Park):
    An ephemeral salt pond found on eastern Bush Key.

Appendix B. Detailed Maps

Loggerhead Key – North

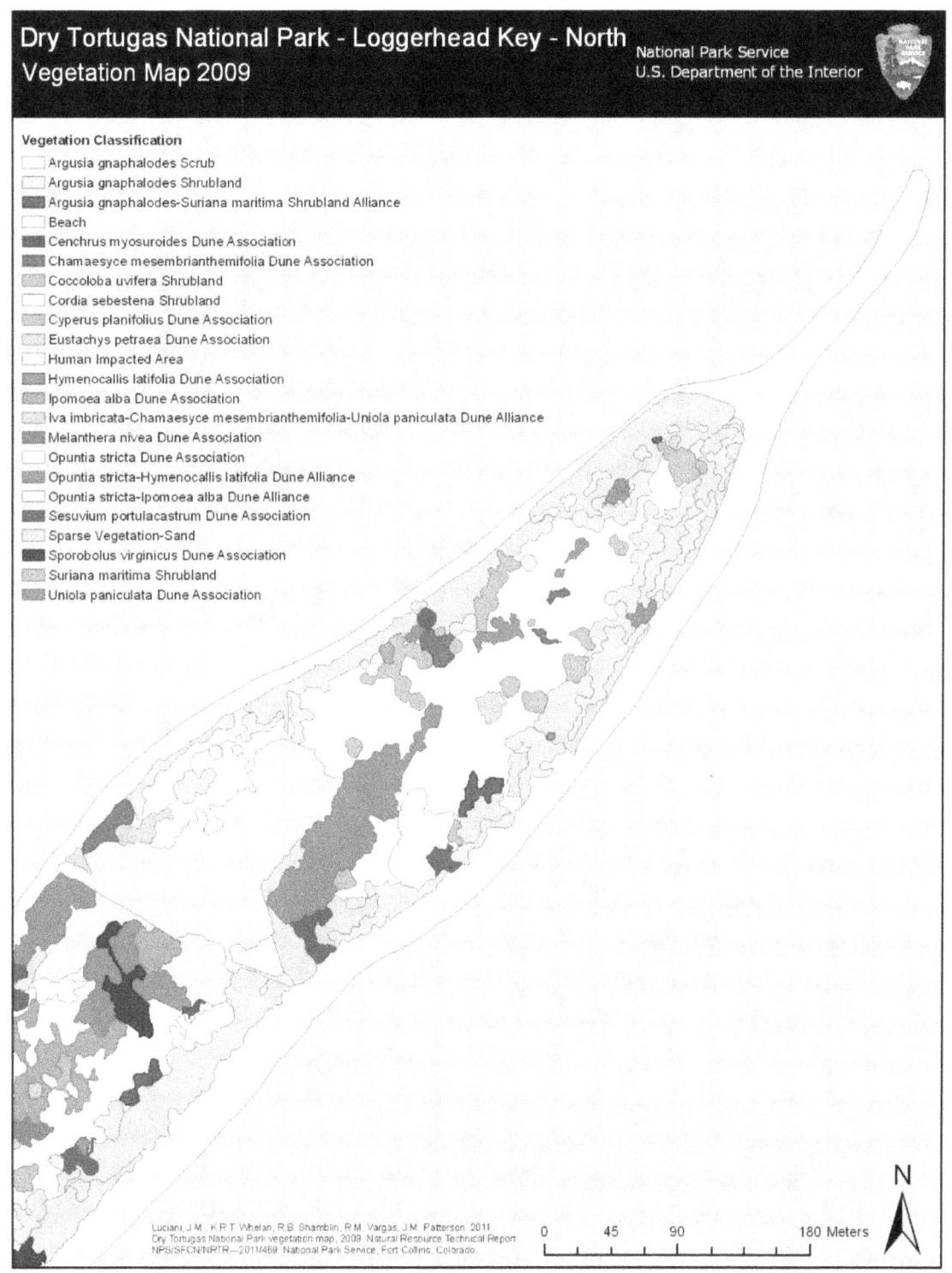

Loggerhead Key – South

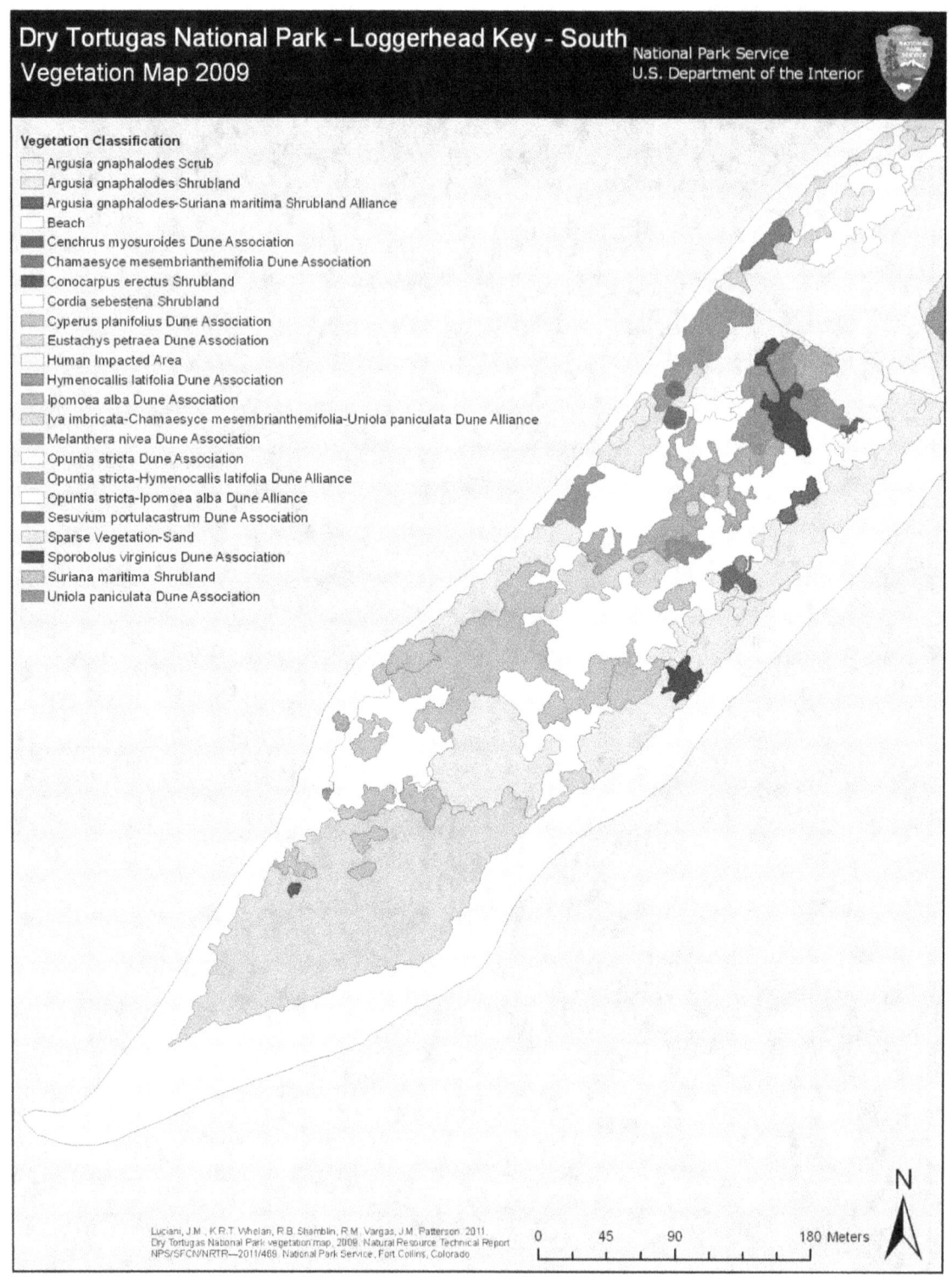

Bush Key – West

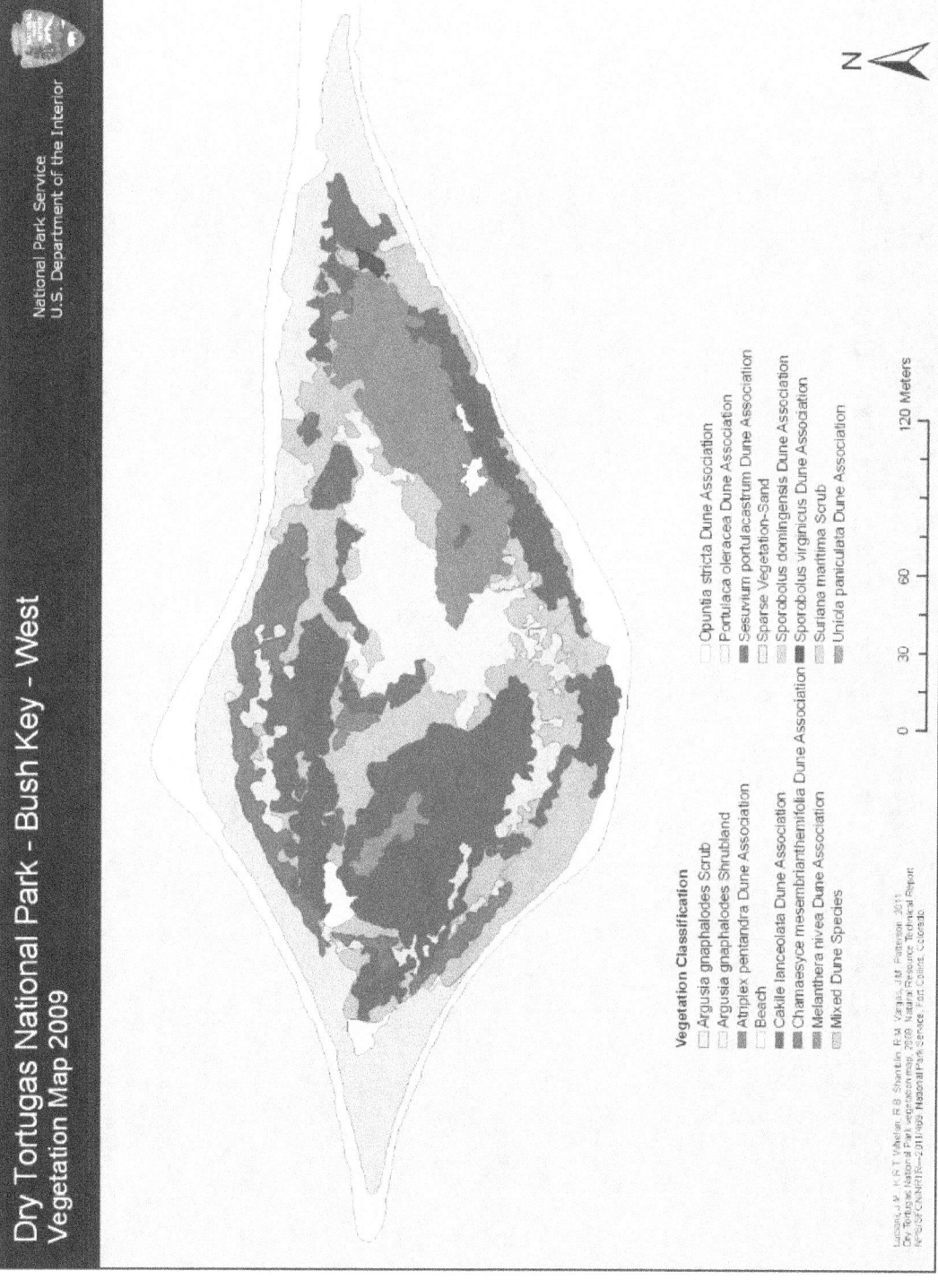

Dry Tortugas National Park – Bush Key – West
Vegetation Map 2009

National Park Service
U.S. Department of the Interior

Vegetation Classification

☐ Argusia gnaphalodes Scrub
☐ Argusia gnaphalodes Shrubland
▨ Atriplex pentandra Dune Association
☐ Beach
▨ Cakile lanceolata Dune Association
▨ Chamaesyce mesembrianthemifolia Dune Association
▨ Melanthera nivea Dune Association
▨ Mixed Dune Species

☐ Opuntia stricta Dune Association
☐ Portulaca oleracea Dune Association
▨ Sesuvium portulacastrum Dune Association
☐ Sparse Vegetation-Sand
▨ Sporobolus domingensis Dune Association
▨ Sporobolus virginicus Dune Association
▨ Suriana maritima Scrub
▨ Uniola paniculata Dune Association

0   30   60   120 Meters

N

Lidsey, J. P., K. R. T. Whelan, R. B. Shamblin, R. M. Vargas, J. M. Patterson. 2011.
Dry Tortugas National Park vegetation map 2009. Natural Resource Technical Report.
NPS/SFCN/NRTR—2011/485. National Park Service. Fort Collins, Colorado.

Bush Key – East

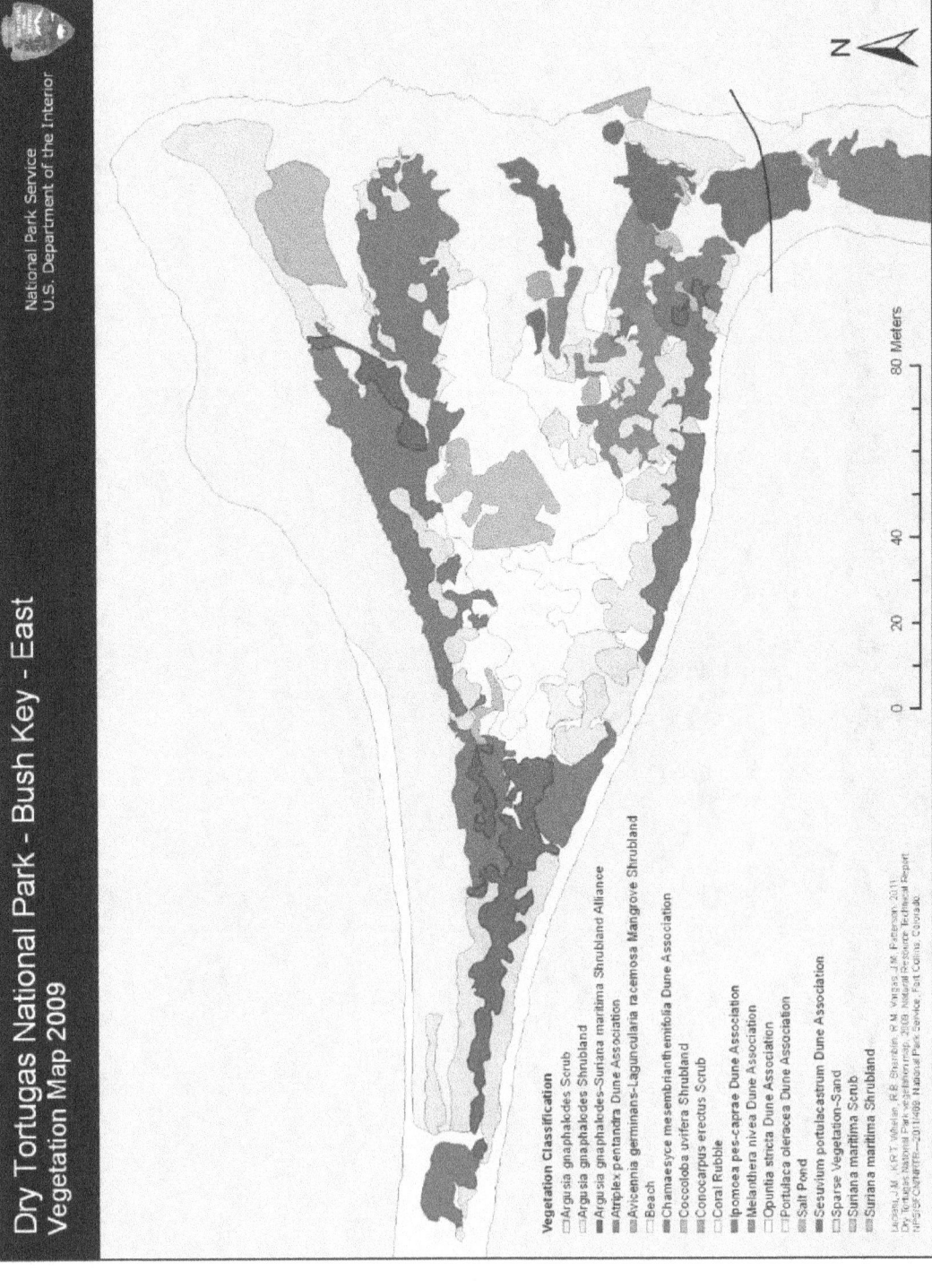

Dry Tortugas National Park - Bush Key - East
Vegetation Map 2009

National Park Service
U.S. Department of the Interior

Vegetation Classification

- Argusia gnaphalodes Scrub
- Argusia gnaphalodes Shrubland
- Argusia gnaphalodes–Suriana maritima Shrubland Alliance
- Atriplex pentandra Dune Association
- Avicennia germinans-Laguncularia racemosa Mangrove Shrubland
- Beach
- Chamaesyce mesembrianthemifolia Dune Association
- Coccoloba uvifera Shrubland
- Conocarpus erectus Scrub
- Coral Rubble
- Ipomoea pes-caprae Dune Association
- Melanthera nivea Dune Association
- Opuntia stricta Dune Association
- Portulaca oleracea Dune Association
- Salt Pond
- Sesuvium portulacastrum Dune Association
- Sparse Vegetation–Sand
- Suriana maritima Scrub
- Suriana maritima Shrubland

Larsen, J.M., K.R.T. Whelan, R.R. Shamblin, R.M. Vargas, J.M. Patterson. 2011.
Dry Tortugas National Park vegetation map, 2009. Natural Resource Technical Report
NPS/SFCN/NRTR—2011/489 National Park Service. Fort Collins, Colorado.

Long Key

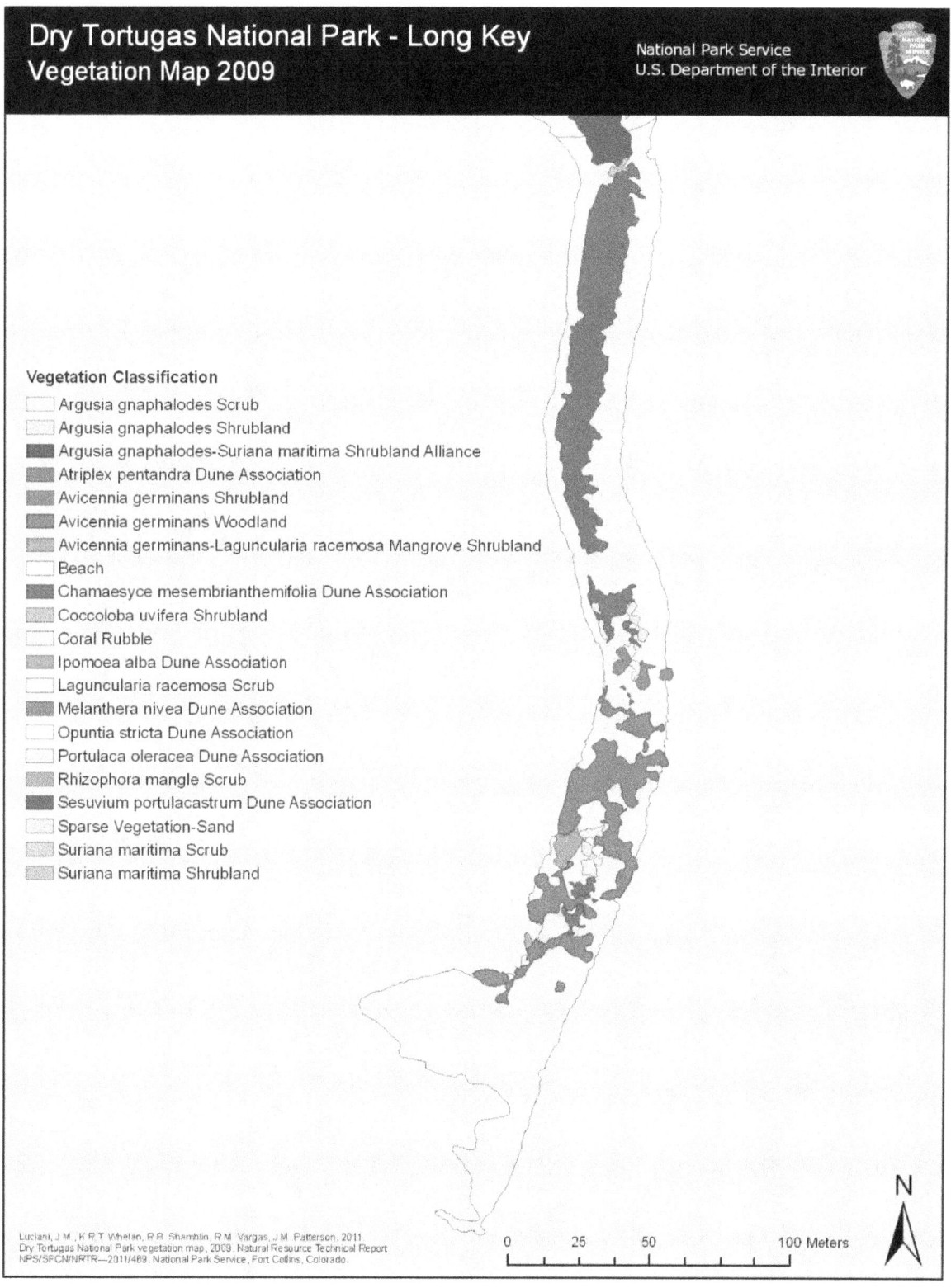

Appendix C. Historical Maps

The following historical maps assisted in determining historical vegetation trends and are included for comparison purposes.

Millspaugh (1907) Historical Maps

Loggerhead Key (as surveyed by Lansing in 1904)

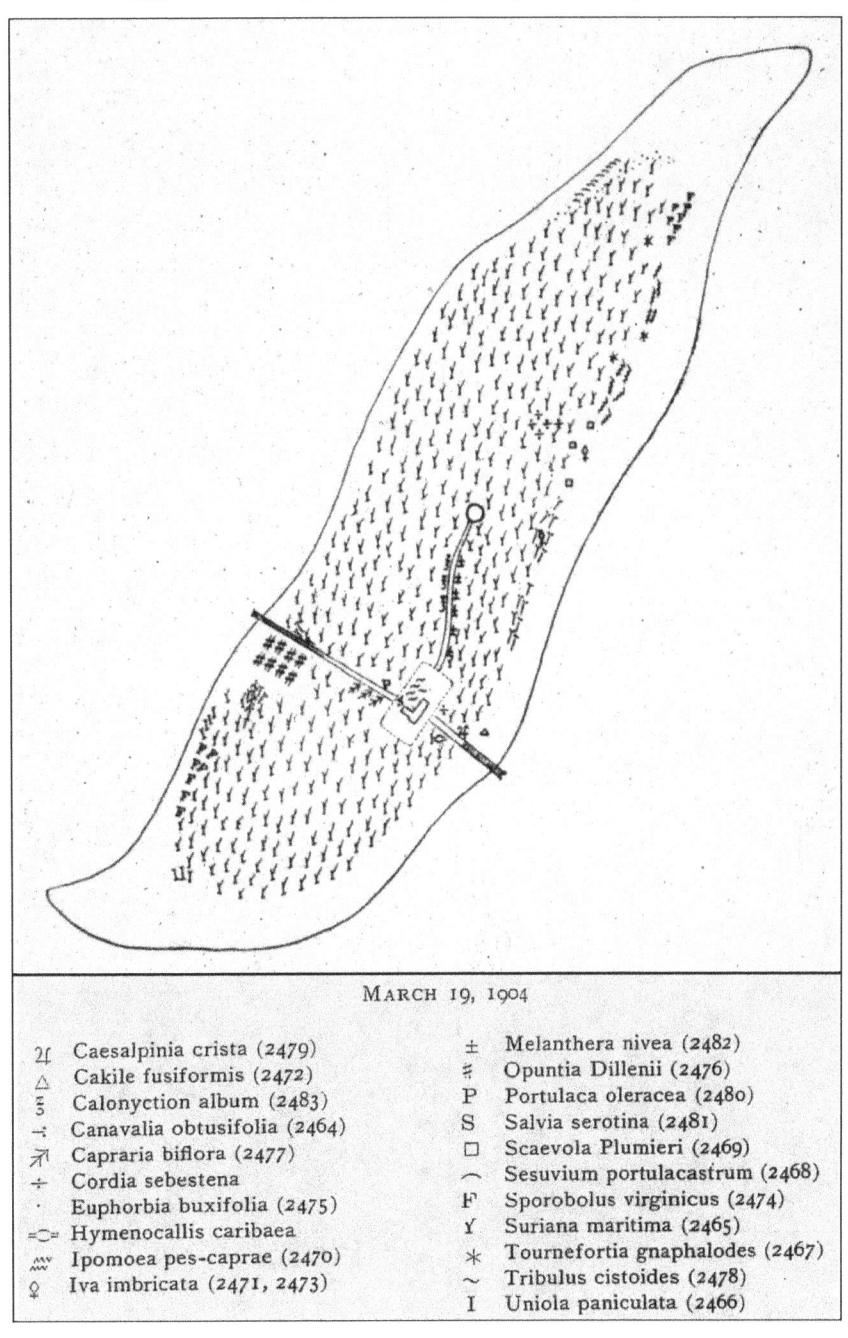

MARCH 19, 1904

♃	Caesalpinia crista (2479)	±	Melanthera nivea (2482)
△	Cakile fusiformis (2472)	≈	Opuntia Dillenii (2476)
ƺ	Calonyction album (2483)	P	Portulaca oleracea (2480)
⊣	Canavalia obtusifolia (2464)	S	Salvia serotina (2481)
⫝̸	Capraria biflora (2477)	□	Scaevola Plumieri (2469)
÷	Cordia sebestena	⌢	Sesuvium portulacastrum (2468)
·	Euphorbia buxifolia (2475)	F	Sporobolus virginicus (2474)
=○=	Hymenocallis caribaea	Y	Suriana maritima (2465)
⩙	Ipomoea pes-caprae (2470)	✳	Tournefortia gnaphalodes (2467)
♀	Iva imbricata (2471, 2473)	∼	Tribulus cistoides (2478)
		I	Uniola paniculata (2466)

Hospital Key (as surveyed by Lansing in 1904)

MARCH 21, 1904

·	Euphorbia buxifolia (2493, 2494)
ᴬꟺ	Ipomoea pes-caprae (2497)
♀	Iva imbricata (2496)
⌒	Sesuvium portulacastrum (2495)
I	Uniola paniculata (2498)

Garden Key (as surveyed by Lansing in 1904)

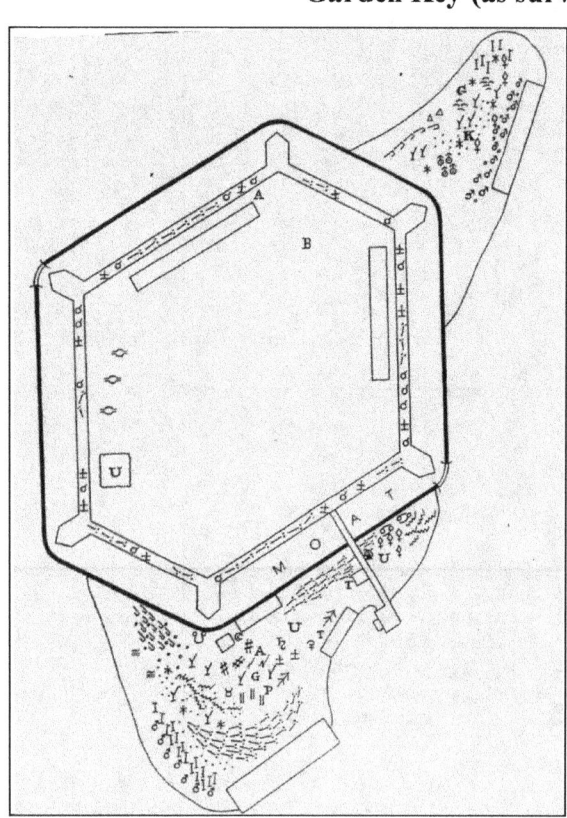

MARCH 22, 1904

ℂ	Amaranthus viridis (2521)	ᴧᴧᴧ	Ipomoea pes-caprae (2518)
🜨	Argemone leiocarpa (2531)	♀	Iva imbricata (2520)
♉	Atriplex cristata (2522)	≅	Lithophila vermicularis (2527)
⩔	Bidens leucantha (2506)	±	Melanthera nivea (2505)
♉	Boerhaavia viscosa (2530)	♯	Opuntia Dillenii (2537)
△	Cakile fusiformis (2517, 2526)	⊐	Paspalum distichum (2528)
⊣	Canavalia obtusifolia (2516)	P	Portulaca oleracea (2503)
⊼	Capraria saxifragaefolia (2501)	T	Sesbania sericea (2519)
♌	Cenchrus echinatus (2512)	⌒	Sesuvium portulacastrum (2524)
♂	Cenchrus tribuloides (2511)	A	Sida carpinifolia (2515, 2535)
°	Cyperus brunneus (2529)	B	Sida diffusa (2534)
♄	Euphorbia adenoptera (2502)	U	Sonchus oleraceus (2499, 2533)
·	Euphorbia buxifolia (2523)	G	Sporobolus purpurascens (2507-8)
♂	Euphorbia havanensis (2536)	Ỿ	Suriana maritima (2532)
⌇	Eustachys petraea (2504)	K	Syntherisma fimbriatum (2510)
‖	Heliotropium curassavicum (2509)	✱	Tournefortia gnaphalodes (2513)
⌔	Hymenocallis caribaea (2514)	I	Uniola paniculata (2525)
		😳	Valerianodes jamaicensis (2500)

98

Bowman (1918) Historical Maps

Loggerhead Key (as surveyed by Bowman in 1915-16)

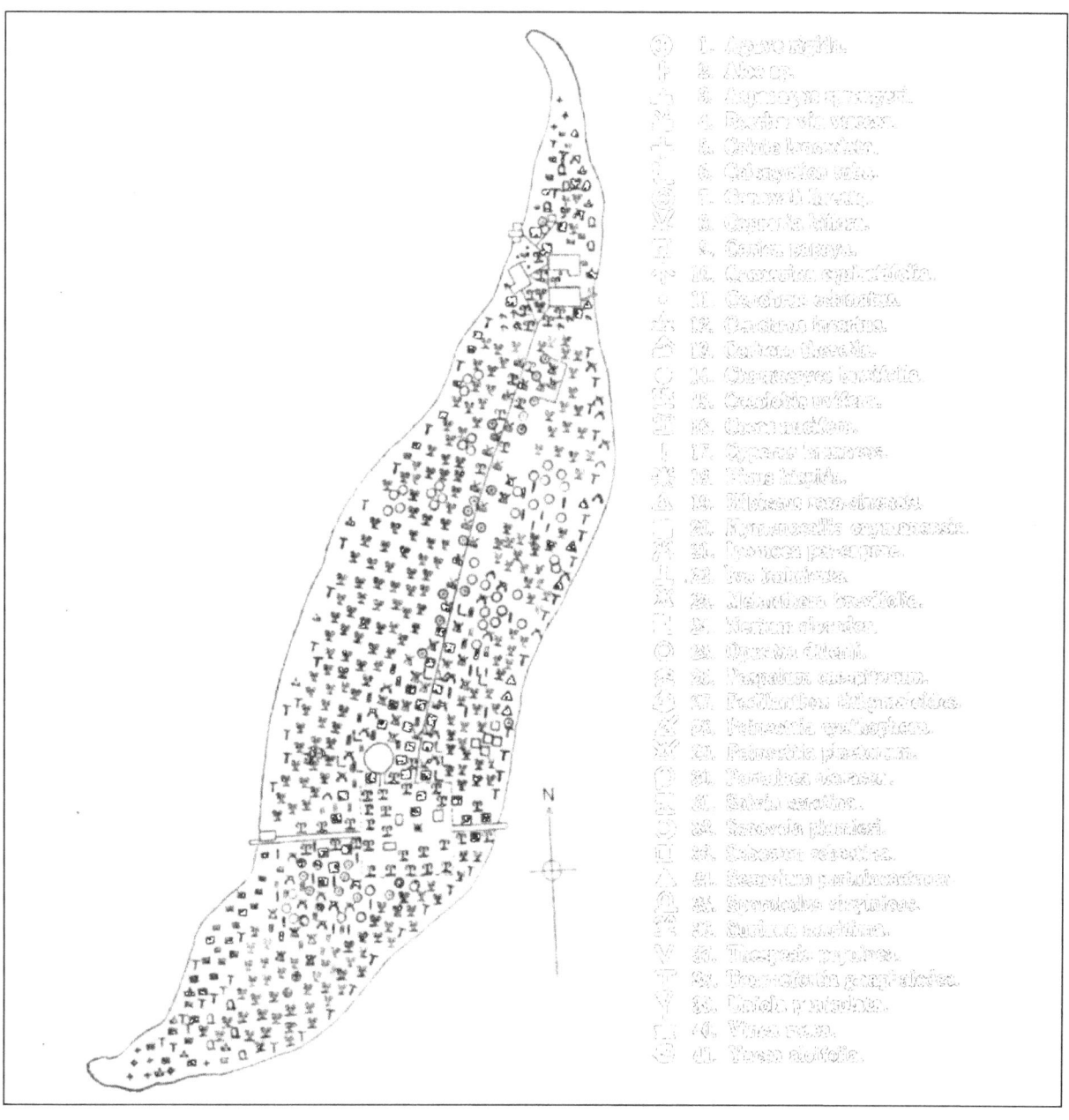

Garden Key (as surveyed by Bowman in 1915-16)

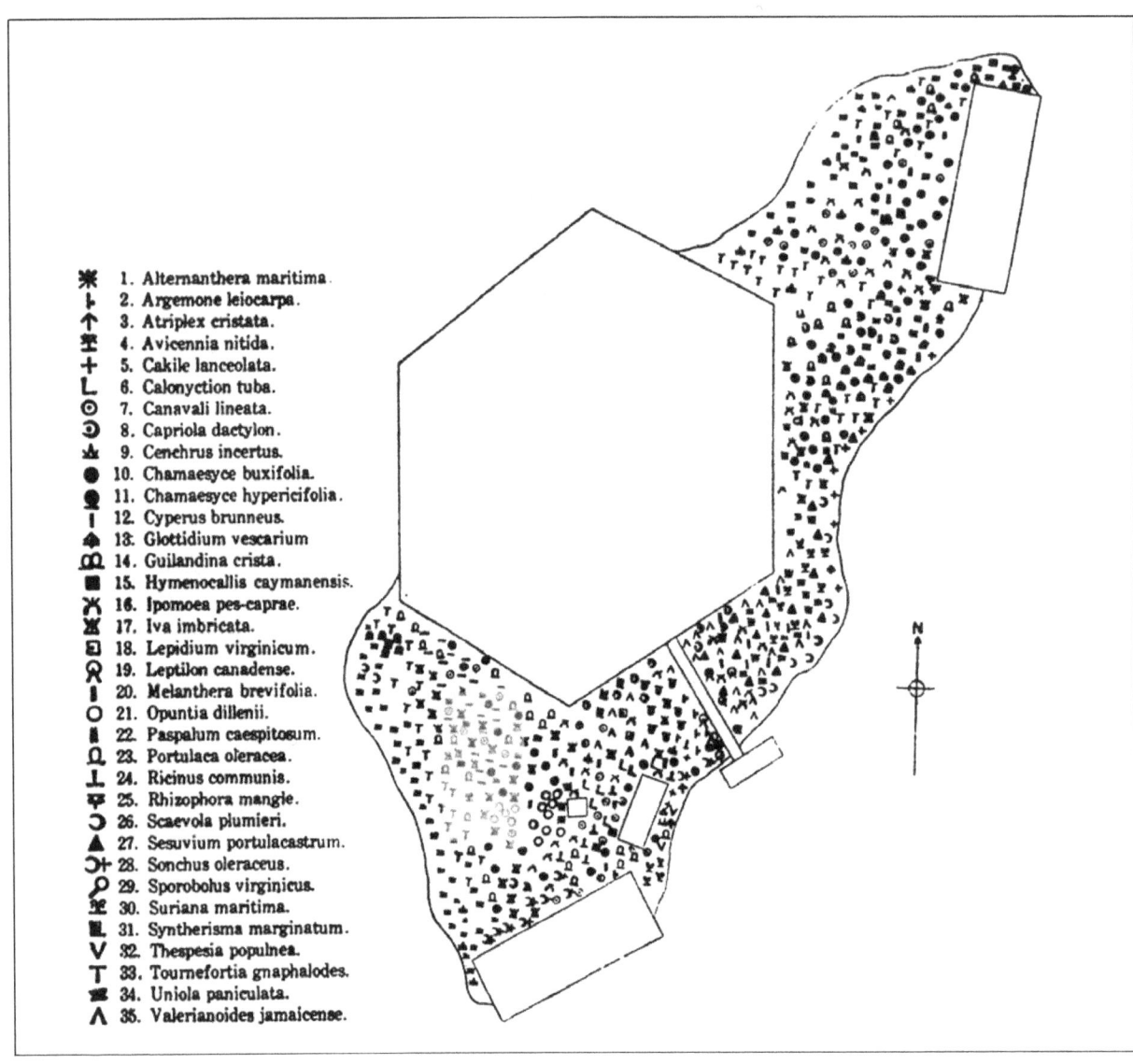

1. Alternanthera maritima.
2. Argemone leiocarpa.
3. Atriplex cristata.
4. Avicennia nitida.
5. Cakile lanceolata.
6. Calonyction tuba.
7. Canavali lineata.
8. Capriola dactylon.
9. Cenchrus incertus.
10. Chamaesyce buxifolia.
11. Chamaesyce hypericifolia.
12. Cyperus brunneus.
13. Glottidium vescarium
14. Guilandina crista.
15. Hymenocallis caymanensis.
16. Ipomoea pes-caprae.
17. Iva imbricata.
18. Lepidium virginicum.
19. Leptilon canadense.
20. Melanthera brevifolia.
21. Opuntia dillenii.
22. Paspalum caespitosum.
23. Portulaca oleracea.
24. Ricinus communis.
25. Rhizophora mangle.
26. Scaevola plumieri.
27. Sesuvium portulacastrum.
28. Sonchus oleraceus.
29. Sporobolus virginicus.
30. Suriana maritima.
31. Syntherisma marginatum.
32. Thespesia populnea.
33. Tournefortia gnaphalodes.
34. Uniola paniculata.
35. Valerianoides jamaicense.

Bush and Long Key (as surveyed by Bowman in 1915-16)

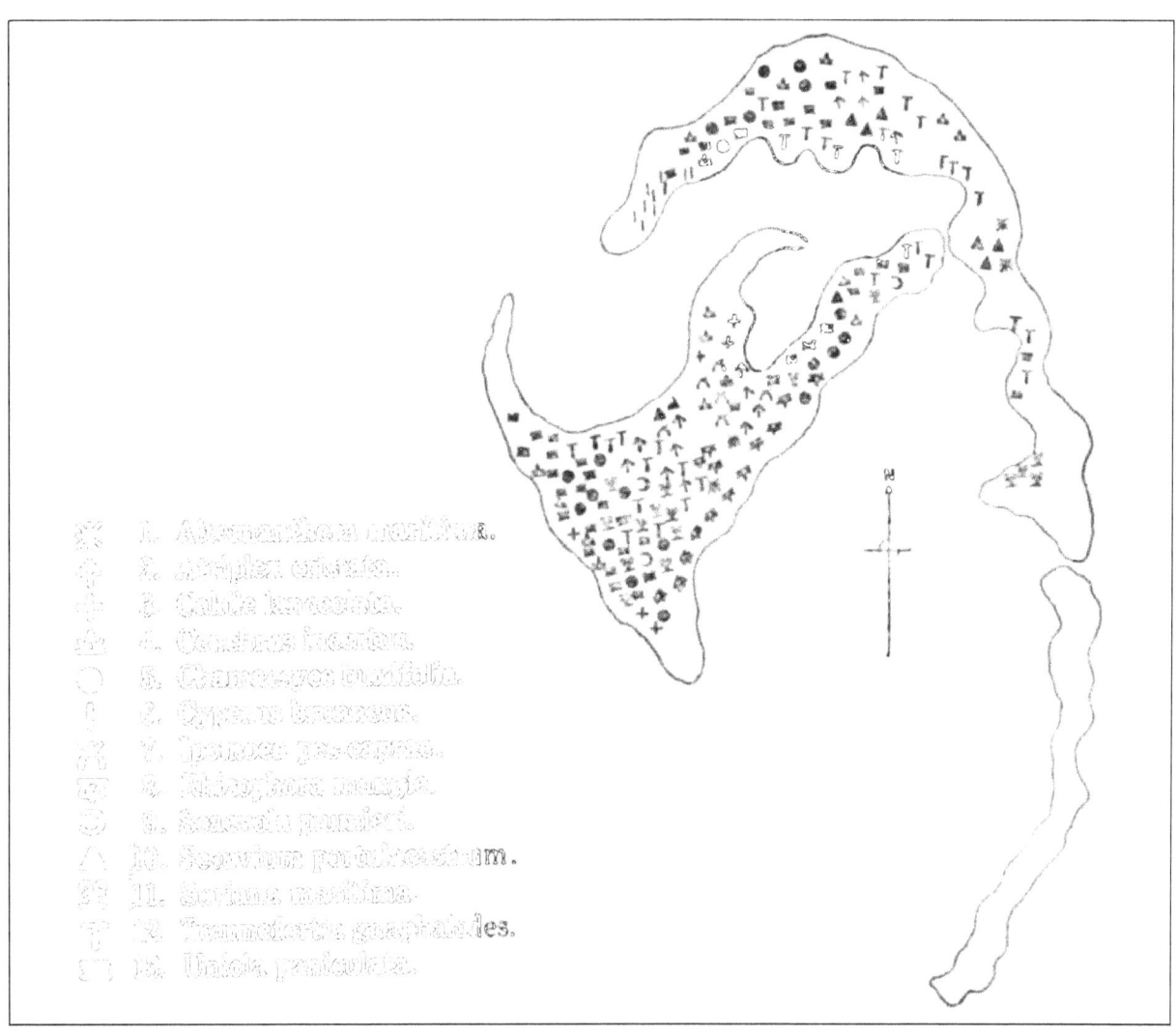

1. Alternanthera maritima.
2. Atriplex arenaria.
3. Cakile lanceolata.
4. Cenchrus incertus.
5. Chamaesyce mesembryanthemifolia.
6. Cyperus brunneus.
7. Ipomoea pes-caprae.
8. Rhabdadenia biflora.
9. Sesuvium portulacastrum.
10. Scaevola plumieri.
11. Sporobolus virginicus.
12. Tournefortia gnaphalodes.
13. Uniola paniculata.

Hospital Key (left) and Middle Key (right) (as surveyed by Bowman in 1915-16)

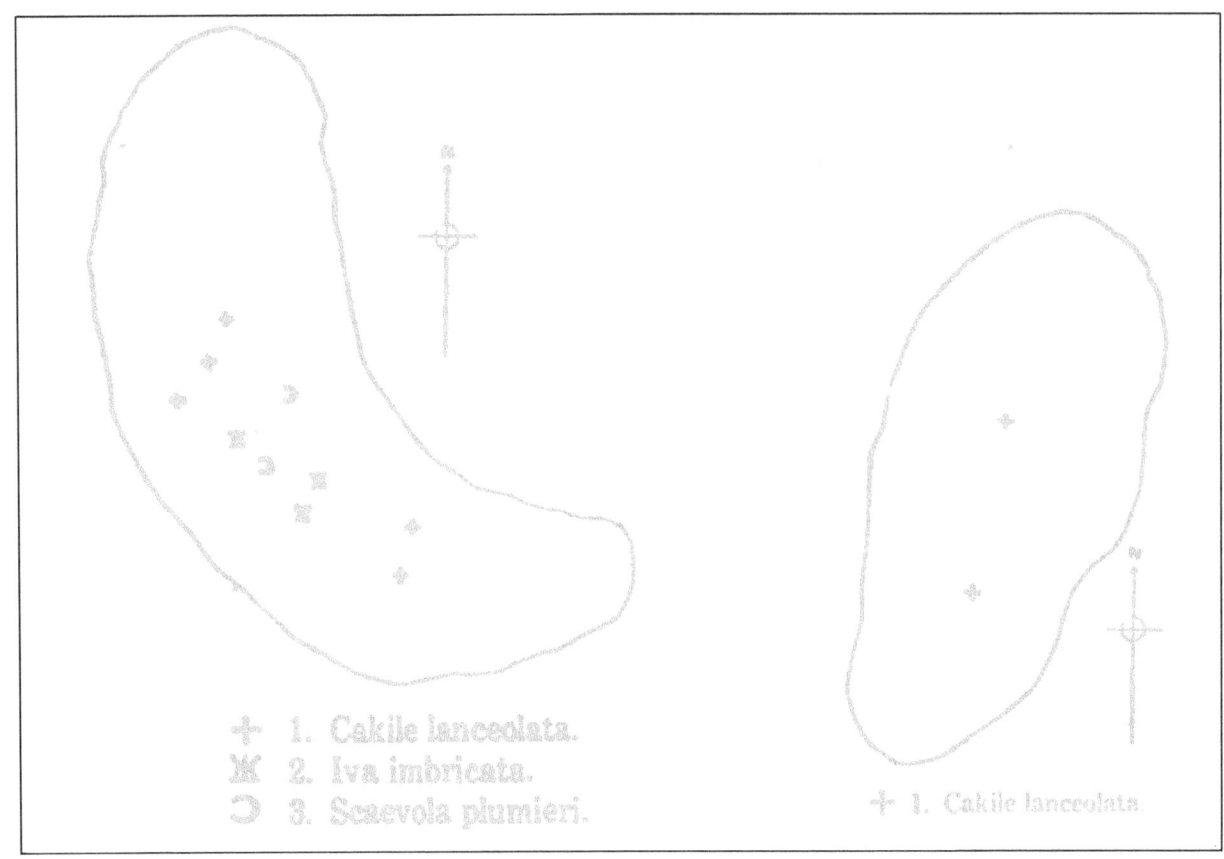

East Key (as surveyed by Bowman in 1915-16)

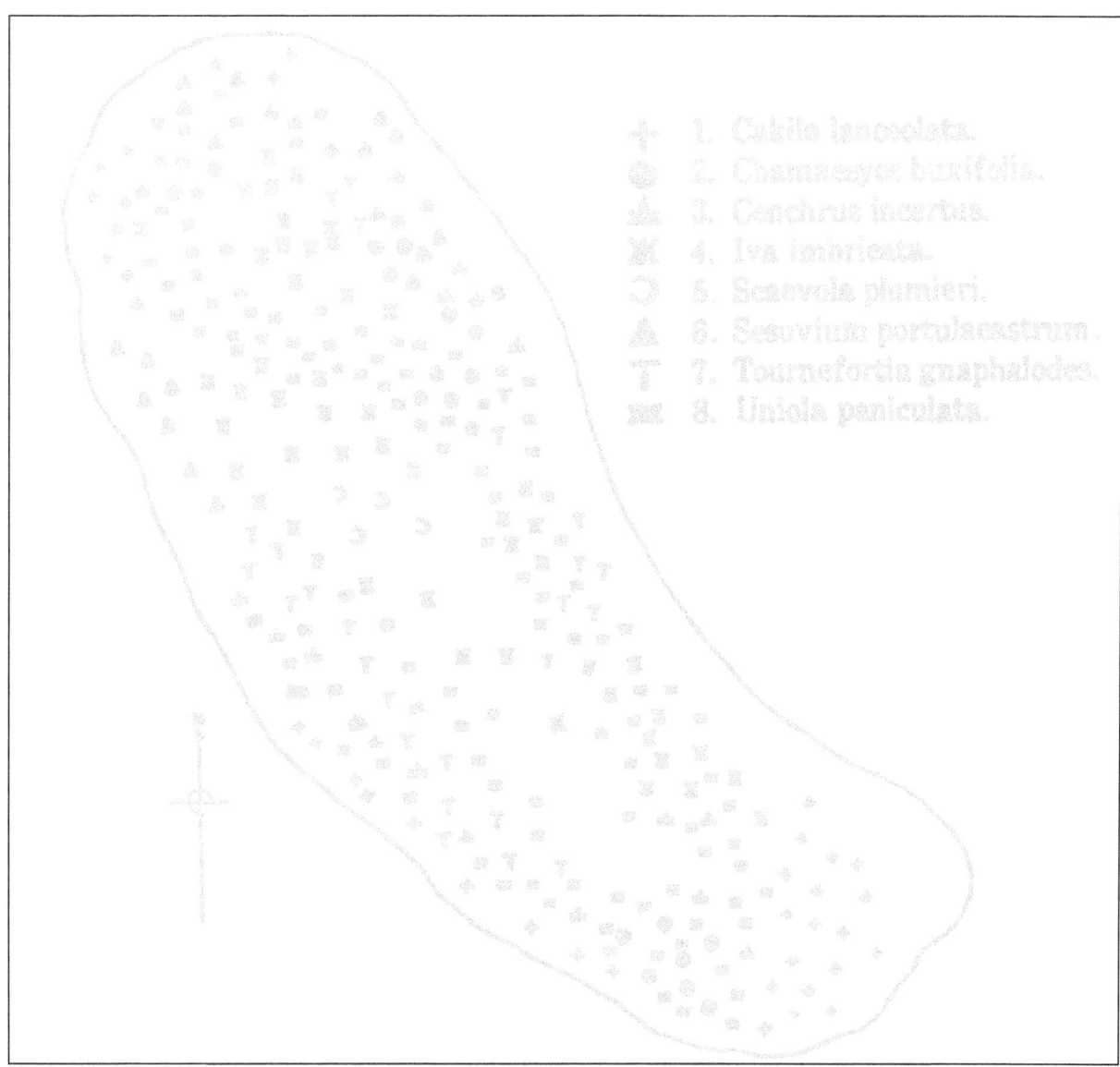

Davis (1942) Historical Maps

Loggerhead, Garden, Bush, and Long Key (as surveyed by Davis in 1937)

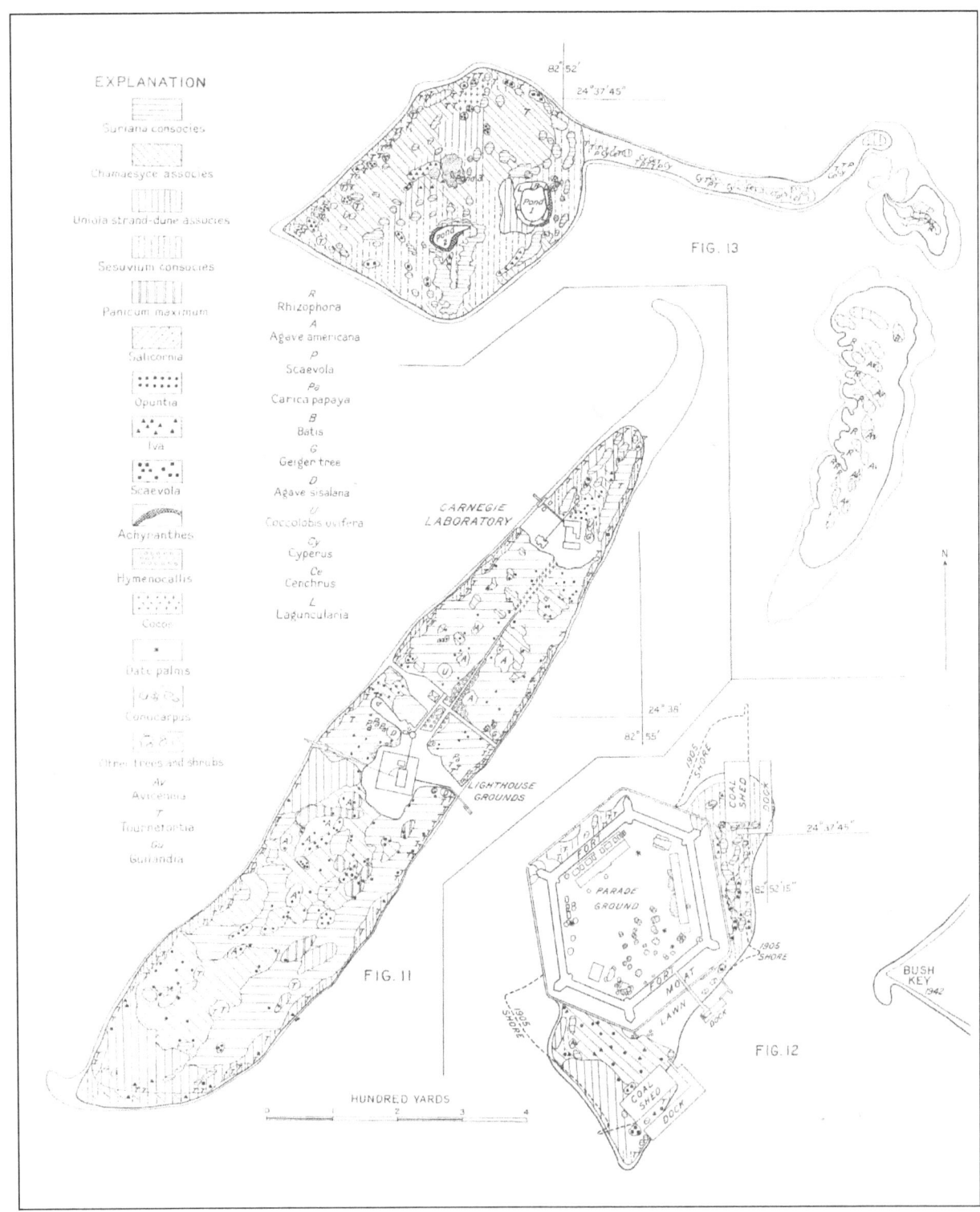

Stoddart and Fosberg (1981) Historical Maps

Loggerhead Key (as surveyed by Stoddart in 1977)

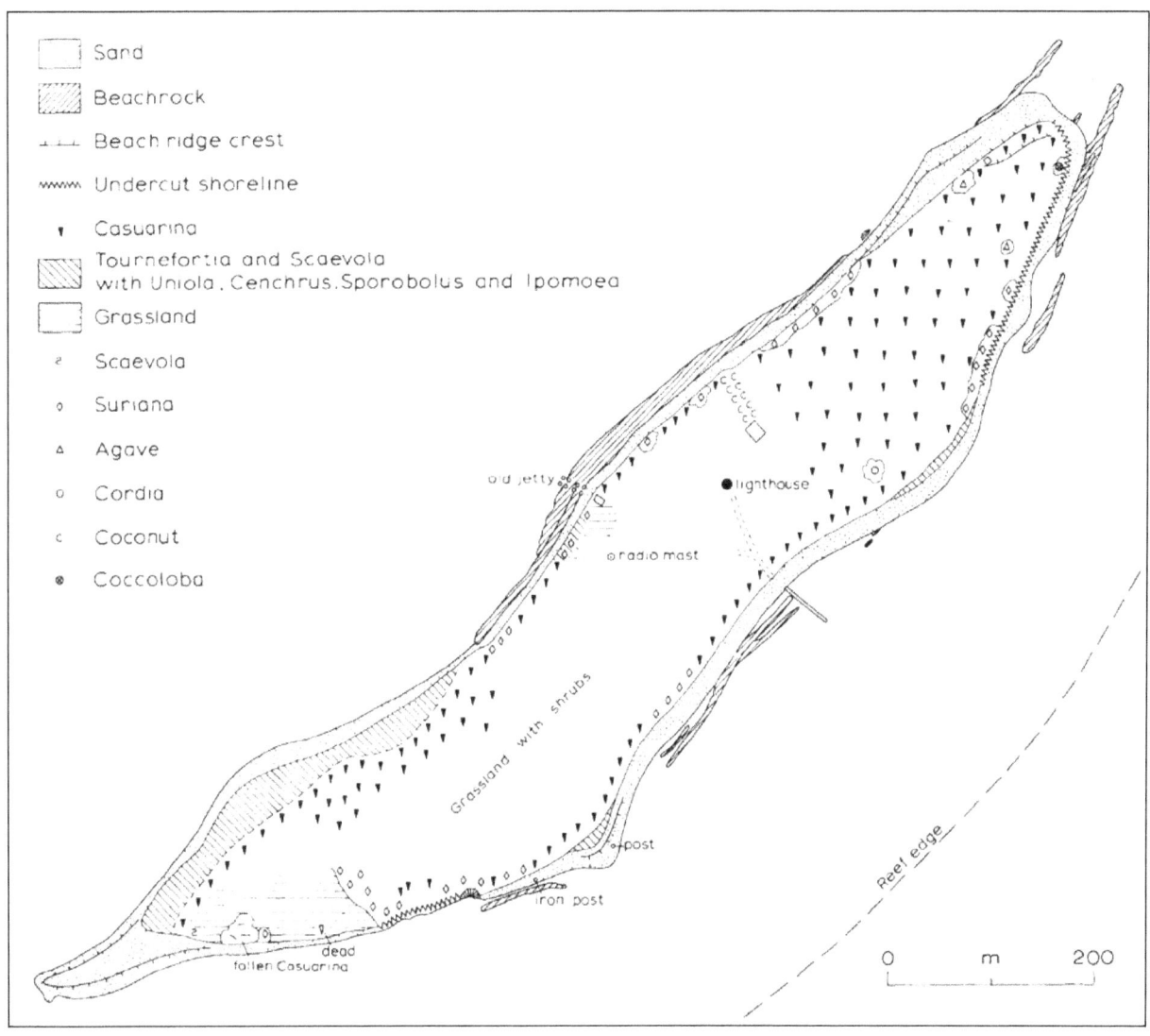

Bush Key and Long Key (as surveyed by Stoddart in 1977)

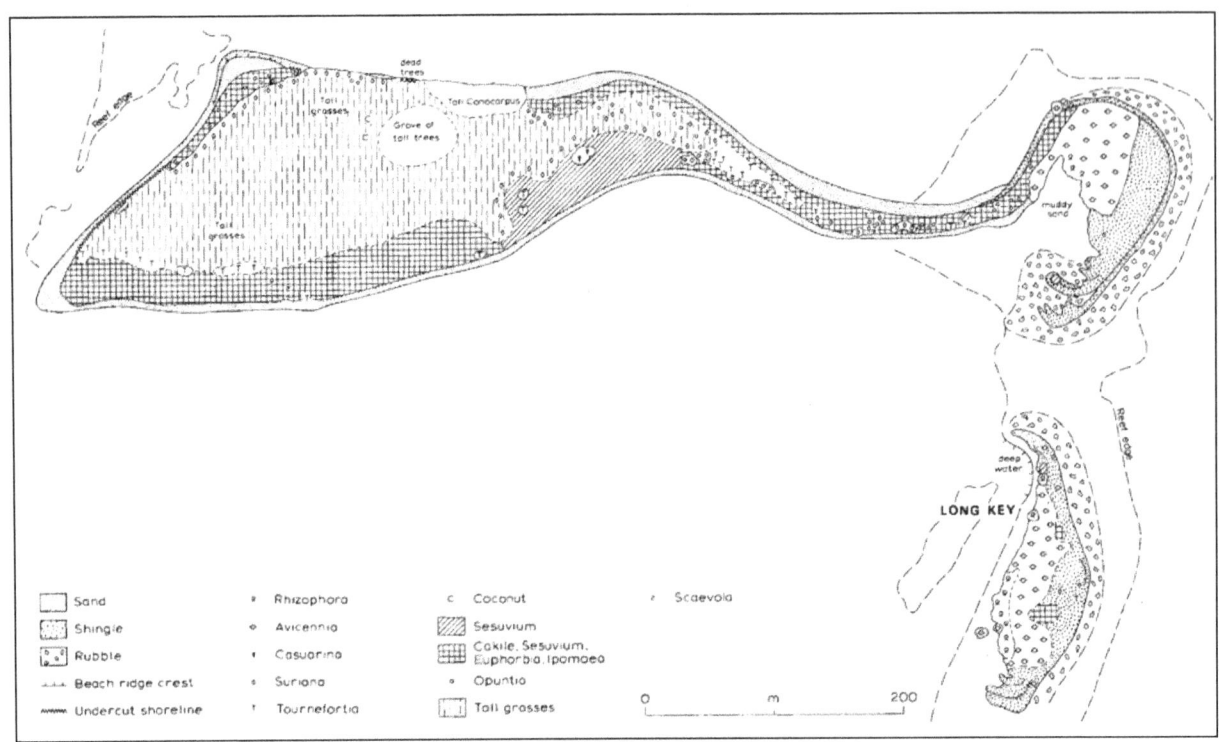

Hospital Key (as surveyed by Stoddart in 1977)

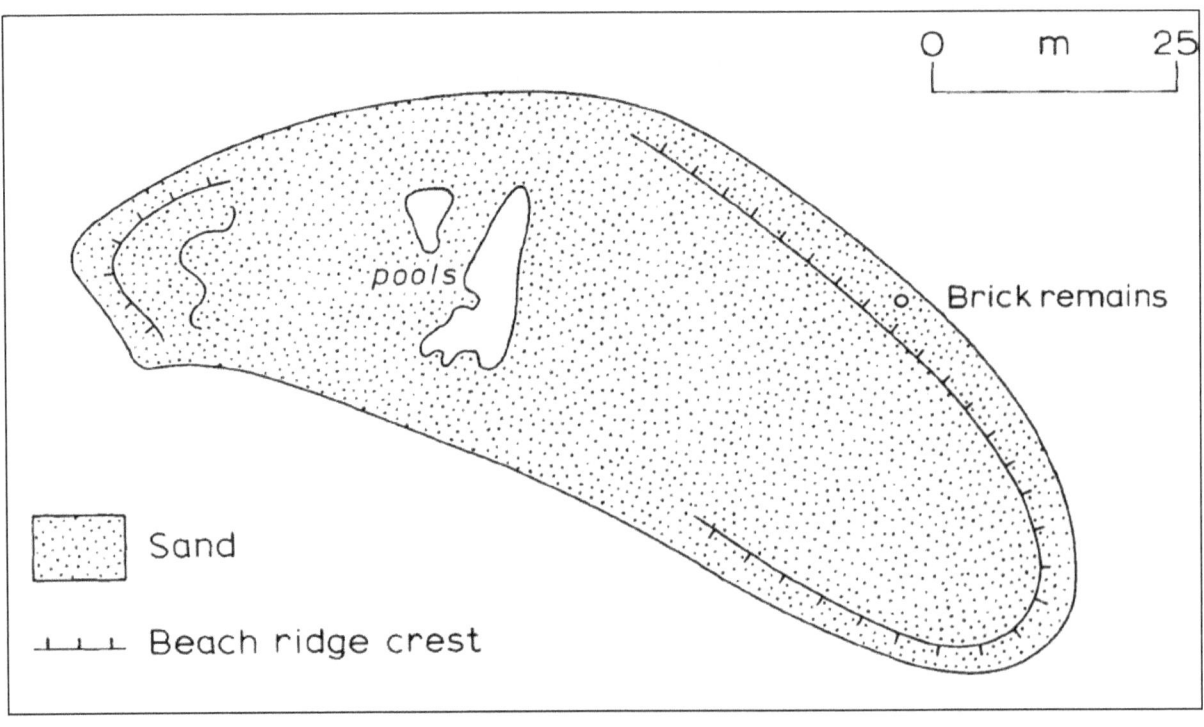

East Key (as surveyed by Stoddart in 1977)

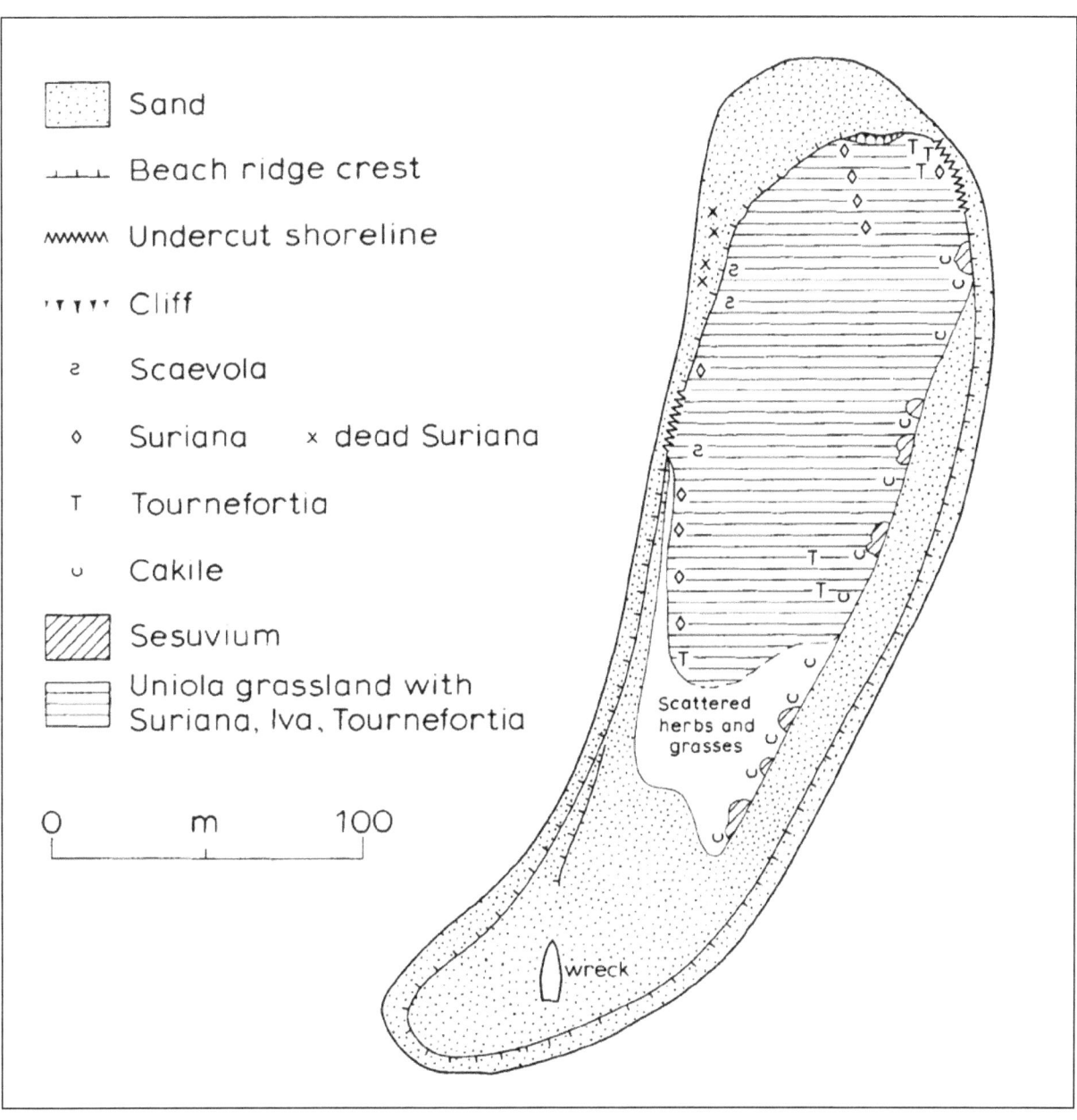

Sand

Beach ridge crest

Undercut shoreline

Cliff

Scaevola

Suriana   × dead Suriana

Tournefortia

Cakile

Sesuvium

Uniola grassland with
Suriana, Iva, Tournefortia

0   m   100

Scattered
herbs and
grasses

wreck

Everglades National Park (1993) Historical Map

Loggerhead Key (1993)

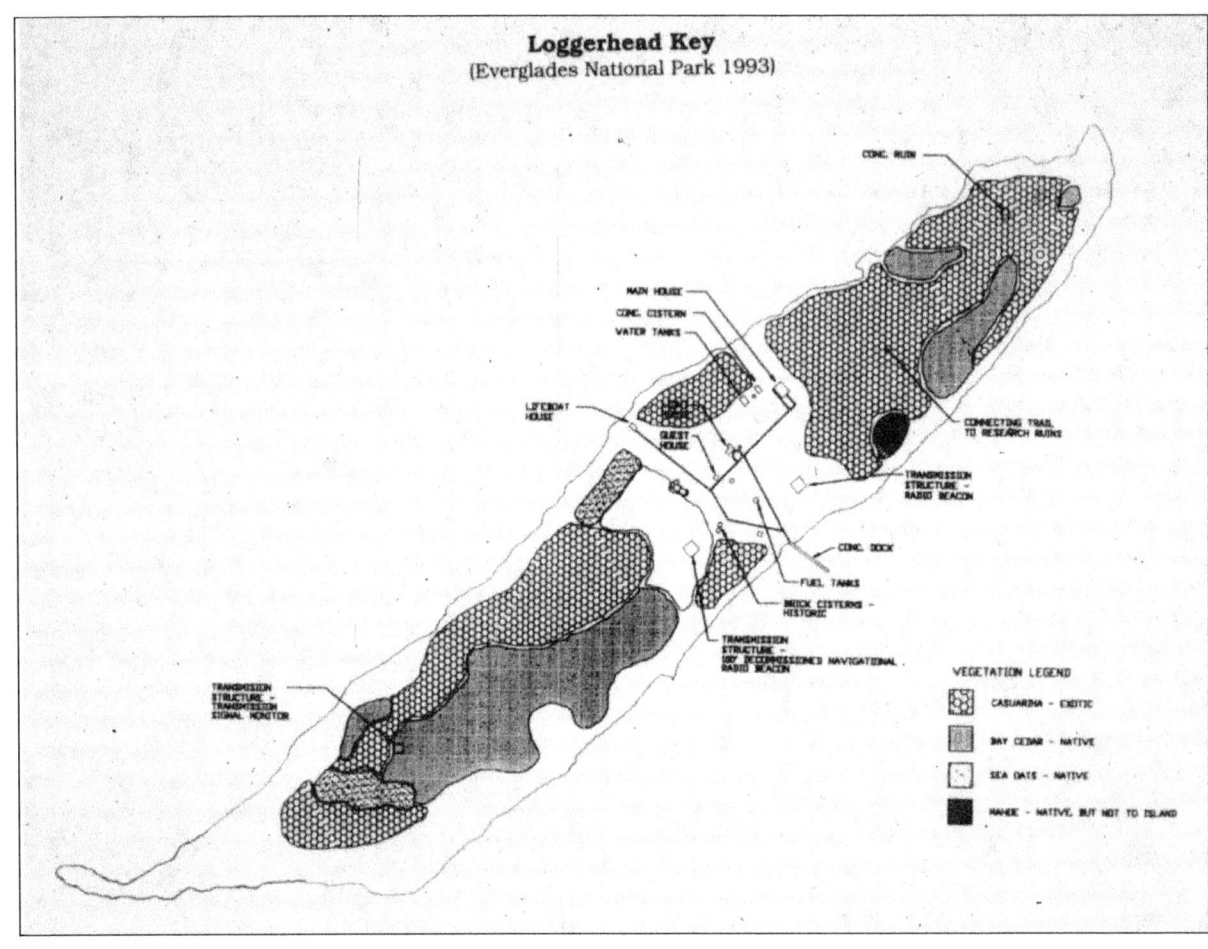

Appendix D. Field Data Sheet

DRTO Vegetation Mapping Data Sheet							
Island:				Observers:			
Date	60 CSx Unit #	GPS Mark #	Polygon/ Point #	Veg Type	Pictures	Species	Comments

NPS 364/108143, July 2011

www.ingramcontent.com/pod-product-compliance
Lightning Source LLC
Chambersburg PA
CBHW081108290526
45795CB00006B/2037